The Amorous Prince by Aphra Behn

Aphra Behn was a prolific and well established writer but facts about her remain scant and difficult to confirm. What can safely be said though is that Aphra Behn is now regarded as a key English playwright and a major figure in Restoration theatre

Aphra was born into the rising tensions to the English Civil War. Obviously a time of much division and difficulty as the King and Parliament, and their respective forces, came ever closer to conflict.

There are claims she was a spy, that she travelled abroad, possibly as far as Surinam.

By 1664 her marriage was over (though by death or separation is not known but presumably the former as it occurred in the year of their marriage) and she now used Mrs Behn as her professional name.

Aphra now moved towards pursuing a more sustainable and substantial career and began work for the King's Company and the Duke's Company players as a scribe.

Previously her only writing had been poetry but now she would become a playwright. Her first, "The Forc'd Marriage", was staged in 1670, followed by "The Amorous Prince" (1671). After her third play, "The Dutch Lover", Aphra had a three year lull in her writing career. Again it is speculated that she went travelling again, possibly once again as a spy.

After this sojourn her writing moves towards comic works, which prove commercially more successful. Her most popular works included "The Rover" and "Love-Letters Between a Nobleman and His Sister" (1684–87).

With her growing reputation Aphra became friends with many of the most notable writers of the day. This is The Age of Dryden and his literary dominance.

From the mid 1680's Aphra's health began to decline. This was exacerbated by her continual state of debt and descent into poverty.

Aphra Behn died on April 16th 1689, and is buried in the East Cloister of Westminster Abbey. The inscription on her tombstone reads: "Here lies a Proof that Wit can never be Defence enough against Mortality." She was quoted as stating that she had led a "life dedicated to pleasure and poetry."

Index of Contents
ARGUMENT
SOURCE
THEATRICAL HISTORY
THE AMOROUS PRINCE - PROLOGUE.
DRAMATIS PERSONÆ
MEN.
WOMEN.
SCENE, The Court of Florence.
ACT I
SCENE I. The Chamber of Cloris.
SCENE II. A Grove.

SCENE III. The Apartment of Antonio
SCENE IV. The Same.
ACT II
SCENE I. The Apartment of Frederick.
SCENE II. Antonio's House.
SCENE III. The Street.
SCENE IV. Antonio's House.
SCENE V. A Chamber in Alberto's House.
ACT III
SCENE I. A Room in Salvator's House.
SCENE II. A Street.
SCENE III. A Wood.
ACT IV
SCENE I. Antonio's House.
SCENE II. A Street.
SCENE III. Frederick's Chamber.
SCENE IV. A Street.
SCENE V. Antonio's House.
ACT V
SCENE I. Laura's Chamber.
SCENE II. A Grove.
SCENE III. The Lodgings of Curtius.
EPILOGUE,
APHRA BEHN – A SHORT BIOGRAPHY
APHRA BEHN – A CONCISE BIBLIOGRAPHY
THE DORSET SQUARE THEATRE – A SHORT HISTORY

ARGUMENT

Frederick, 'the Amorous Prince,' a mercurial young gallant, son to the Duke of Florence, under a solemn promise of marriage debauches Cloris, sister to his friend and confidant, Curtius. The girl has always led a secluded country life, and this relationship is unknown to the Prince, who upon hearing the praises of Laura, beloved by Curtius, straightway resolves to win this lady also. Laura's brother Lorenzo, a wanton madcap favourite of Frederick's, gladly effects the required introduction, and when Curtius interrupts and forbids, Salvator, father to Laura and Lorenzo, promptly turns the quondam lover out of the house. Lorenzo himself is idly pursuing Clarina, wife to a certain Antonio, an abortive intrigue carried on to his own impoverishment, but the enrichment of Isabella, Clarina's woman, a wench who fleeces him unmercifully. Antonio being of a quaint and jealous humour would have his friend Alberto make fervent love to Clarina, in order that by her refusals and chill denials her spotless conjugal fidelity may be proved. However, Ismena, Clarina's sister, appears in a change of clothes as the wife, and manifold complications ensue, but eventually all is cleared and Ismena accepts Alberto, whom she has long loved; not before Isabella, having by a trick compelled Lorenzo to declare himself her husband, enforces the bargain. Cloris, meanwhile, disguised as a boy under the name of Philibert, attaches herself to Frederick, first succouring him when he is wounded in a duel by Curtius. Curtius to avenge his wrongs disguises himself, and as a pandar entices Frederick into a snare by promises of supplying the amorous Prince with lovely cyprians. Bravos, however, are in waiting, but these prove to be in the service of Antonio, who appears with Alberto and their friends, completely frustrating the plot, whilst Clarina, Ismena, and other ladies have acted the courtezans to deceive Curtius, and at the same time read the Prince a salutary lesson. He profits so much by this experience that he takes Cloris, whose sex is discovered, to be his bride, whilst Laura bestows her hand on the repentant and forgiven Curtius.

SOURCE

Mrs. Behn has taken her episode of Antonio's persuading Alberto to woo Clarina from Robert Davenport's fine play, The City Night-Cap (Quarto 1661, but licensed 24 October, 1624) where Lorenzo induces Philippo to test Abstemia in the same way. Astrea, however, has considerably altered the conduct of the intrigue. Bullen (The Works of Robert Davenport, 1890) conclusively and exhaustively demonstrates that Davenport made use of Greene's popular Philomela; the Lady Fitzwater's Nightingale (1592, 1615, and 1631), wherein Count Philippo employs Giovanni Lutesio to 'make experience of his wife's [Philomela's] honesty', rather than was under any obligation to Cervantes' Curioso Impertinente, Don Quixote, Book IV, ch. vi-viii. Read, Dunlop, and Hazlitt all had express'd the same opinion. The Spanish tale turns upon the fact of Anselmo, the Curious Impertinent, enforcing his friend Lothario to tempt his wife Camilla. Such a theme, however, is common, and with variations is to be found in Italian novelle. Recent authorities are inclined to suggest that the plot of Beaumont and Fletcher's The Coxcomb (1610), much of which runs on similar lines, is not founded on Cervantes. Southerne, in his comedy, The Disappointment; or, The Mother in Fashion (1684) and 'starch Johnny Crowne' in The Married Beau (1694), both comedies of no little wit and merit, are patently indebted to The Curious Impertinent. Cervantes had also been used three quarters of a century before by Nat Field in his Amends for Ladies (Quarto, 1618), where Sir John Loveall tries his wife in an exactly similar manner to Lorenzo, Count Philippo and Anselmo.

The amours of the Florentine court are Mrs. Behn's own invention; but the device by which Curtius ensnares Frederick is not unlike Vendice and Hippolito's trapping of the lecherous old Duke in The Revenger's Tragedy (Quarto, 1607), albeit the saturnine Tourneur gives the whole scene a far more terrible and tragic catastrophe.

In January, 1537, Lorenzino de Medici having enticed Duke Alessandro of Florence to his house under pretext of an assignation with a certain Caterina Ginori, after a terrible struggle assassinated him with the aid of a notorious bravo. Several plays have been founded upon this history.

Notable amongst them are Shirley's admirable tragedy, The Traitor (licensed May, 1631, Quarto 1635) and in later days de Musset's Lorenzaccio (1834).

The Mask in Act V of The Amorous Prince is in its purport most palpably akin to the Elizabethans.

THEATRICAL HISTORY

The Amorous Prince was produced by the Duke's Company in the spring of 1671 at their Lincoln's Inn Fields theatre, whence they migrated in November of the same year to the magnificent new house in Dorset Garden. No performers' names are given to the comedy, which met with a very good reception. It seems to have kept the boards awhile, but there is no record of any particular revival.

THE AMOROUS PRINCE.

PROLOGUE.

Well! you expect a Prologue to the Play,
And you expect it too Petition-way;
With Chapeau bas beseeching you t' excuse
A damn'd Intrigue of an unpractis'd Muse;
Tell you it's Fortune waits upon your Smiles,
And when you frown, Lord, how you kill the whiles!
Or else to rally up the Sins of th' Age,
And bring each Fop in Town upon the Stage;
And in one Prologue run more Vices o'er,
Than either Court or City knew before:
Ah! that's a Wonder which will please you too,
But my Commission's not to please you now.
First then for you grave Dons, who love no Play
But what is regular, Great Johnson's way;
Who hate the Monsieur with the Farce and Droll,
But are for things well said with Spirit and Soul;
'Tis you I mean, whose Judgments will admit
No Interludes of fooling with your Wit;
You're here defeated, and anon will cry,
'Sdeath! wou'd 'twere Treason to write Comedy.
So! there's a Party lost; now for the rest,
Who swear they'd rather hear a smutty Jest
Spoken by Nokes or Angel, than a Scene
Of the admir'd and well penn'd Cataline;
Who love the comick Hat, the Jig and Dance,
Things that are fitted to their Ignorance:
You too are quite undone, for here's no Farce
Damn me! you'll cry, this Play will be mine A----
Not serious, nor yet comick, what is't then?
Th' imperfect issue of a lukewarm Brain:
'Twas born before its time, and such a Whelp;
As all the after-lickings could not help.
Bait it then as ye please, we'll not defend it,
But he that disapproves it, let him mend it.

DRAMATIS PERSONÆ

MEN.
Frederick, Son to the Duke.
Curtius, his Friend.
Lorenzo, a rich extravagant Lord, a kind of Favourite to Frederick.
Salvator, Father to Lorenzo and Laura.
Antonio, a Nobleman of Florence.
Alberto, his dear Friend, a Nobleman also.
Pietro, Man to Curtius.
Galliard, Servant to the Prince.

Guilliam, Man to Cloris, a Country-fellow.
Valet to Antonio.

WOMEN.

Clarina, Wife to Antonio.
Ismena, Sister to Antonio, in love with Alberto.
Laura, Sister to Lorenzo, in love with Curtius.
Cloris, Sister to Curtius, disguis'd like a Country Maid, in love with Frederick.
Isabella, Woman to Clarina.
Lucia, Maid to Cloris.
Pages and Musick.

SCENE, The Court of Florence.

ACT I.

SCENE I. The Chamber of Cloris.

Enter Cloris drest in her Night Attire, with Frederick dressing himself.

CLORIS - And will you leave me now to Fears,
Which Love it self can hardly satisfy?
But those, and that together sure will kill me,
If you stay long away.

FREDERICK - My Dear, 'tis almost day, and we must part;
Should those rude Eyes 'mongst whom thou dwell'st perceive us,
'Twould prove unhappy both to thee and me.

CLORIS - And will you, Sir, be constant to your Vows?

FREDERICK - Ah Cloris! do not question what I've sworn;
If thou would'st have it once again repeated,
I'll do't. By all that's good, I'll marry thee;
By that most Holy Altar, before which we kneel'd,
When first I saw the brightest Saint that e'er ador'd it;
I'll marry none but thee, my dearest Cloris.

CLORIS - Sir, you have said enough to gain a credit
With any Maid, though she had been deceiv'd
By some such Flatteries as these before.
I never knew the pains of Fear till now;   [Sighs.
And you must needs forgive the Faults you make,
For had I still remain'd in Innocence,
I should have still believ'd you.

FREDERICK - Why, dost thou not, my Love?

CLORIS - Some doubts I have, but when I look on you,
Though I must blush to do so, they all vanish;
But I provide against your absence, Sir.

FREDERICK - Make no provision, Cloris, but of Hope,
Prepare thy self against a Wedding day,
When thou shalt be a little Deity on Earth.

CLORIS - I know not what it is to dwell in Courts,
But sure it must be fine, since you are there;
Yet I could wish you were an humble Shepherd,
And knew no other Palace than this Cottage;
Where I would weave you Crowns, of Pinks and Daisies,
And you should be a Monarch every May.

FREDERICK - And, Cloris, I could be content to sit
With thee, upon some shady River's Bank,
To hear thee sing, and tell a Tale of Love.
For these, alas! I could do any thing;
A Sheep-hook I could prize above a Sword;
An Army I would quit to lead a Flock,
And more esteem that Chaplet wreath'd by thee,
Than the victorious Bays:
All this I could, but, Dear, I have a Father,
Whom for thy sake, to make thee great and glorious,
I would not lose my Int'rest with.
But, Cloris, see, the unkind day approaches,
And we must kiss and part.

CLORIS - Unkind it is indeed, may it prove so
To all that wish its presence,
And pass as soon away,
That welcome Night may re-assume its place,
And bring you quickly back.

FREDERICK - With great impatience I'll expect that Hour,
That shall conduct me in its Shades to thee;
Farewel.

CLORIS - Farewel, Sir, if you must be gone.   [Sighs.

FREDERICK - One Kiss, and then indeed I will be gone.   [Kisses her.
A new blown Rose kist by the Morning Dew,
Has not more natural Sweetness.
Ah Cloris! can you doubt that Heart,
To whom such Blessings you impart?
Unjustly you suspect that Prize,
Won by such Touches and such Eyes.
My Fairest, turn that Face away,
Unless I could for ever stay;
Turn but a little while I go.

CLORIS - Sir, I must see the last of you.

FREDERICK - I dare not disobey; adieu till Evening.

[Exit.

Enter Lucia.

CLORIS - How now, Lucia; is my Father up?

LUCIA - No, not a Mouse stirs yet; I have kept a true
Watch all this Night, for I was cruelly afraid
Lest we should have been surpriz'd
Is the Prince gone? but why do I ask,
That may read it in your sad Looks?

CLORIS - Yes, he is gone, and with him too has taken -   [Sighs.

LUCIA - What has he taken? I'll swear you frighten me.

CLORIS - My heart, Lucia.

LUCIA - Your Heart, I am glad 'tis no worse.

CLORIS - Why, what dost think he should have taken?

LUCIA - A thing more hard to have been
Recovered again.

CLORIS - What thing, prithee?

LUCIA - Your Maiden-head.

CLORIS - What's that?

LUCIA - A thing young Gallants long extremely for,
And when they have it too, they say
They care not a Daisy for the Giver.

CLORIS - How comest thou so wise, Lucia?

LUCIA - Oh, the fine Gentleman that comes a-nights
With the Prince, told me so much, and bid me
Be sure never to part with it for fine Words;
For Men would lye as often as they swore;
And so bid me tell you too.

CLORIS - Oh Lucia!

LUCIA - Why do you sigh?

CLORIS - To think if Princes were like common Men,
How I should be undone,
Since I have given him all I had to give;
And who that looks on him can blame my Faith?

LUCIA - Indeed he surpasses Damon far;
But I'ad forgot my self, you are the Prince's Wife;
He said you should be kneel'd to, and ador'd,
And never look'd on but on Holy-days:
That many Maids should wait upon your call,
And strow fine Flowers for you to tread upon.
Musick and Love should daily fill your Ears,
And all your other Senses should be ravish'd
With wonders of each kind great as your Beauty.

CLORIS - Lucia, methinks you have learnt to speak fine things.

LUCIA - I have a thousand more I've heard him say;
Oh, I could listen a whole Night to hear him talk:
But hark, I hear a Noise, the House is up,
And must not find us here.

CLORIS - Lock up this Box of Jewels for me.

LUCIA - Oh rare! what, did these come to night?

CLORIS - Yes, yes, away.

[Exeunt.

SCENE II. A Grove.

Enter Curtius and Pietro.

CURTIUS - I wonder the Prince stays so long;
I do not like these Night-works;
Were I not confident of Cloris's Virtue,
Which shall no more be tempted.
I hear some coming, and hope 'tis he
Pietro, are the Horses ready?   [Exit Pietro.

Enter Frederick.

CURTIUS - Sir, you are welcome from Cloris's Arms.

FREDERICK - With much ado, I am got loose from those fair
Fetters, but not from those of her Beauty;
By these she still inflames me,
In spite of all my humours of Inconstancy;

So soft and young, so fair and innocent,
So full of Air, and yet of Languishment;
So much of Nature in her Heart and Eyes,
So timorous and so kind without disguise:
Such untaught Sweets in every part do move,
As 'gainst my Reason does compel my Love;
Such artless smiles, look so unorder'd too,
Gains more than all the charms of Courts can do;
From Head to Foot, a spotless Statue seems,
As Art, not Nature, had compos'd her Limbs;
So white, and so unblemish'd, oh Curtius!
I'm ravisht beyond Sense when I but think on't;
How much more must my Surprize be,
When I behold these Wonders.

CURTIUS - And have you seen her, Sir, in all this Beauty?
Oh Hell!   [Aside.

FREDERICK - Curtius, I will not hide my Soul from thee;
I have seen all the marvels of that Maid.

CURTIUS - My Soul, learn now the Art of being disguis'd;   [Aside.
'Tis much, my Lord, that one
Bred in such simple Innocence,
Should learn so soon so much of Confidence:
Pray, Sir, what Arts and Cunning do you use?

FREDERICK - Faith, time and importunity refuse no body.

CURTIUS - Is that the way? had you no other Aids?
Made you no promise to her, Sir, of Marriage?

FREDERICK - Oh, yes, in abundance, that's your only bait,
And though they cannot hope we will perform it,
Yet it secures their Honour and my Pleasure.

CURTIUS - Then, Sir, you have enjoy'd her?

FREDERICK - Oh, yes, and gather'd Sweets
Would make an Anchoret neglect his Vow,
And think he had mistook his way to future bliss,
Which only can be found in such Embraces;
'Twas hard to gain, but, Curtius, when once Victor,
Oh, how the joys of Conquest did enslave me!

CURTIUS - But, Sir, methinks 'tis much that she should yield,
With only a bare promise that you'd marry her.

FREDERICK - Yes, there was something more - but

CURTIUS - But, what, Sir, you are not married.

FREDERICK - Faith, yes, I've made a Vow,
And that you know would go as far with any other Man.

CURTIUS - But she it seems forgot you were the Prince?

FREDERICK - No, she urg'd that too,
And left no Arguments unus'd
Might make me sensible of what I did;
But I was fixt, and overcame them all,
Repeating still my Vows and Passions for her,
Till in the presence of her Maid and Heaven
We solemnly contracted.

CURTIUS - But, Sir, by your permission, was it well?

FREDERICK - What wouldst thou have him do
That's all on fire, and dies for an Enjoyment?

CURTIUS - But having gain'd it, do you love her still?

FREDERICK - Yes, yes, extremely,
And would be constant to the Vows I've made,
Were I a Man, as thou art of thy self;
But with the aid of Counsels I must chuse,
And what my Soul adores I must refuse.

CURTIUS - This Passion, Sir, Possession will destroy,
And you'l love less, the more you do enjoy.

FREDERICK - That's all my hope of cure; I'll ply that game,
And slacken by degrees th' unworthy flame.

CURTIUS - Methinks, my Lord, it had more generous been
To've check'd that flame when first it did begin,
E'er you the slighted Victory had won,
And a poor harmless Virgin quite undone:
And what is worse, you've made her love you too.

FREDERICK - Faith, that's the greater mischief of the two;
I know to such nice virtuous Souls as thine,
My juster Inclination is a Crime:
But I love Pleasures which thou canst not prize,
Beyond dull gazing on thy Mistress Eyes,
The lovely Object which enslaves my Heart,
Must yet more certain Cures than Smiles impart:
And you on Laura have the same design.

CURTIUS - Yes, Sir, when justify'd by Laws Divine.

FREDERICK - Divine! a pleasant Warrant for your Sin,

Which being not made, we ne'er had guilty been.
But now we speak of Laura,
Prithee, when is't that I shall see that Beauty?

CURTIUS - Never, I hope. [Aside.] I know not, Sir,
Her Father still is cruel, and denies me,
What she and I have long made suit in vain for:
But, Sir, your Interest might prevail with him,
When he shall know I'm one whom you esteem;
He will allow my flame, and my address,
He whom you favour cannot doubt Success.

FREDERICK - This day I will begin to serve thee in it.

CURTIUS - Sir, 'twill be difficult to get access to her,
Her Father is an humorous old Man,
And has his fits of Pride and Kindness too.

FREDERICK - Well, after Dinner I will try my Power,
And will not quit his Lodgings till I've won him.

CURTIUS - I humbly thank you, Sir.

FREDERICK - Come let us haste, the Day comes on apace.   [Ex. FREDERICK -

CURTIUS - I'll wait upon you, Sir.
Oh Cloris, thou'rt undone, false amorous Girl;
Was it for this I bred thee in obscurity,
Without permitting thee to know what Courts meant,
Lest their too powerful Temptation
Might have betray'd thy Soul?
Not suffering thee to know thy Name or Parents,
Thinking an humble Life might have secur'd thy Virtue:
And yet I should not hate thee for this Sin,
Since thou art bred in so much Innocence,
Thou couldst not dream of Falsity in Men:
Oh, that it were permitted me to kill this Prince,
This false perfidious Prince;
And yet he knows not that he has abus'd me.
When did I know a Man of so much Virtue,
That would refuse so sweet and soft a Maid?
No, he is just and good, only too much misled
By Youth and Flattery;
And one to whom my Soul is ty'd by Friendship;
Yet what's a Friend, a name above a Sister?
Is not her Honour mine?
And shall not I revenge the loss of it?
It is but common Justice.
But first I'll try all gentle means I may,
And let him know that Cloris is my Sister;
And if he then persevere in his Crime,

I'll lay my Interest and my Duty by,
And punish him, or with my Honour die.   [Exit.

SCENE III. The Apartment of Antonio

Enter Lorenzo pulling in of Isabella.

LORENZO - Nay, nay, Isabella, there's no avoiding me now,
You and I must come to a parley.
Pray what's the reason
You took no notice of me,
When I came with so civil an address too?

ISABELLA - Can you ever think to thrive in an Amour,
When you take notice of your Mistress,
Or any that belongs to her, in publick,
And when she's a married Woman too?

LORENZO - Good Isabella, the loser may have leave to speak,
I am sure it has been a plaguy dear Amour to me.

ISABELLA - Let me hear you name that again,
And you shall miss of my Assistance.

LORENZO - Nay, do but hear me a little;
I vow 'tis the strangest thing in the World,
A Man must part from so much Money as I have done,
And be confin'd to Signs and Grimaces only,
To declare his Mind in:
If a Man has a Tongue, let him exercise it, I say,
As long as he pays for speaking.

ISABELLA - Again with your paying for't? I see you are not
To be reclaim'd; farewell -

LORENZO - Stay, good Isabella, stay,
And thou shalt hear not one word of that more,
Though I am soundly urg'd to't.

ISABELLA - Yes, yes, pray count them, do;
I know you long to be at it,
And I am sure you will find you are in Arrears to us.

LORENZO - Say you so, I am not of that opinion: but well,
Let me see, here 'tis, here 'tis
My Bill of Charge for courting Clarina.
[Draws out his Table Book, and reads.

ISABELLA - And here's mine for the returns that have been
Made you; begin, begin.   [Pulls out her Book.

LORENZO - Item, two hundred Crowns to Isabella for undertaking.

ISABELLA - Item, I have promis'd Lorenzo to serve him
In his Amour with all Fidelity.

LORENZO - Well, I own that Debt paid, if you keep
Your word, out with it then   [He crosses that out.
Item, two thousand Crowns in a Bracelet for Clarina;
What say you to that now, Isabella?

ISABELLA - Item, the day after they were presented,
She saluted you with a smile at the Chappel.

LORENZO - And dost thou think it was not dearly bought?

ISABELLA - No Man in Florence should have had it
A Souce cheaper.

LORENZO - Say you so, Isabella? out with it then.   [Crosses it out.
Item, one hundred more to thee for presenting them.

ISABELLA - Which I did with six lyes in your Commendation,
Worth ten Pistoles a piece for the exactness of a Lye;
Write there indebted to me -

LORENZO - Nay then thou dost deserve it:
Rest due to Isabella.   [Writes.
Item, Innumerable Serenades, Night-walks, Affronts
And Fears; and lastly, to the Poets for Songs, and the like.

ISABELLA - All which was recompensed in the excessive
Laughing on you that Day you praunc'd under our
Window on Horse-back, when you made such a
Deal of Capriol and Curvet.

LORENZO - Yes, where I ventur'd my Neck to shew my
Activity, and therefore may be well accompted
Amongst my Losses.

ISABELLA - Then she receiv'd your Presents,
Suffer'd your Serenades, without sending her Foot-men
To break your Pate with the Fiddles.

LORENZO - Indeed that was one of the best Signs;
For I have been a great Sufferer in that kind
Upon the like occasions: but dost thou think
In Conscience that this should satisfy?

ISABELLA - Yes, any reasonable Man in the World, for the
First Month at least; and yet you are still up

With your Expences, as if a Lady of her Quality
Were to be gain'd without them.
Let me hear of your Expences more, and I'll -

LORENZO - Oh sweet Isabella! upon my Knees
I beg thou wilt take no fatal Resolution;
For I protest, as I am a Man of Honour,
And adore thy Sex, thou shalt only see,
Not hear of my Expences more;
And for a small testimony of it, here take this;
There's twenty Pistoles upon Reputation.   [Gives her Money.

ISABELLA - Fy, fy, 'tis not brave, nor generous to name
The Sum, you should have slid it into my Coat,
Without saying what you had done.

LORENZO - What signifies that, mun, as long as 'tis current,
And you have it sure?

ISABELLA - Well, leave the management of your Affairs to me
What shall we do? here's Alberto.

Enter Alberto.

LORENZO - Well, who can help it? I cannot walk invisible.

ALBERTO - Lorenzo, what, making Love to Isabella?

LORENZO - She'l serve, my Lord, for want of a better.

ISABELLA - That's but a coarse Complement.

LORENZO - 'Twill serve to disguise a Truth however.   [Aside to her.
[Ex. Isabella.
Faith, I'll tell you, Sir, 'twas such another Damsel
As this, that sav'd me five hundred Pound once upon a time;
And I have lov'd the whole Tribe of Waiting-women
The better ever since.

ALBERTO - You have reason; how was it?

LORENZO - Why, look you, Sir,
I had made Love a long time to a Lady;
But she shall be nameless,
Since she was of a quality not to be gain'd under
The aforesaid Sum: well, I brought it,
Came pouder'd and perfum'd, and high in expectation.

ALBERTO - Well, Sir.

LORENZO - And she had a very pretty Wench, who was to

Conduct me, and in the dark too;
And, on my Conscience, I e'en fell aboard of her,
And was as well accommodated for my five,
As five Hundred Pounds, and so return'd.

ALBERTO - A great defeat to the Lady the while, a my word.

LORENZO - Ay, she smelt the Plot, and made a Vow to follow
The Italian mode for the future;
And be serv'd in Affairs of that kind by none
But an old Woman.

ALBERTO - 'Twas wittily resolv'd.

LORENZO - Are you for the Presence this Morning?

ALBERTO - No, I have business here with Antonio.

LORENZO - Your Servant, my Lord.   [Exit.

ALBERTO - I do not like this Fellow's being here,
The most notorious Pimp and Rascal in Italy;
'Tis a vile shame that such as he should live,
Who have the form and sense of Man about them,
And in their Action Beast;
And that he thrives by too.

Enter Isabella.

Isabella, is Antonio stirring?

ISABELLA - He is, please your Lordship to walk in.

ALBERTO - You may tell him I wait here:
For I would avoid all opportunity of seeing Clarina.   [Aside.

ISABELLA - My Lord, you need not stand upon Ceremonies.   [Exit Alberto.

Enter Clarina and Ismena, dress'd like one another in everything, laughing and beholding one another.

Dress'd already! now on my conscience
I know not which is which:
Pray God Antonio be not mistaken at night,
For I'll be sworn I am by day-light.

ISMENA - Dost think I may pass thus for Clarina?

ISABELLA - Madam, you are the same to a hair;
Wou'd I might never stir
If I can do any thing but wonder.

CLARINA - But hark, Isabella, if thou shou'dst have
Heard amiss, and that thy information should not be good,
Thou hast defeated us of a design,
Wherein we promise our selves no little pleasure.

ISMENA - Yes, I vow, all the Jest is lost if it be so.

ISABELLA - I doubt 'twill be a true Jest on your side.   [Aside.
I warrant you, Madam, my Intelligence is good;
And to assure you of what I have said,
I dare undertake you shall hear the same over again:
For just now Alberto is come to visit my Lord,
Who I am sure will entertain him with no other stories,
But those of his Jealousy,
And to persuade him to court you.

CLARINA - 'Tis strange, since he set him that Task so long ago,
He would not begin before.

ISMENA - Nay, pray God he begin now;
Sister, he has hitherto took me for thee,
And sometimes his Eyes give me hope of a secret
Fire within, but 'twill not out;
And I am so impatient till he declares himself,
That if he do not do it soon,
I shall e'en tell him who I am;
For perhaps the Wife takes off the appetite,
Which would sharpen upon knowledge of the Virgin.

CLARINA - What then, you'll have all the sport to your self?
But, Ismena, remember my little Revenge on Antonio
Must accompany your Love to Alberto.   [Aside.

ISABELLA - But why this resemblance?
For, Madam, since he never saw you,
And takes Ismena to be you;
Might you not still pass so, without this likeness?

CLARINA - Didst thou not say Antonio left the Court
And City, on purpose to give Alberto the more freedom
To Court me? Whilst he was away, I needed but retire,
And Ismena appear, and 'twould suffice;
But now he is return'd,
He may chance to see them together, en passant, or so,
And this dress will abuse him as well as Alberto;
For without that, this Plot of ours signifies little.

ISMENA - Ay, truly, for my part, I have no other design
Than doing my Sister a service.

ISABELLA - The Plot is very likely to thrive I see,
Since you are so good at dissembling.

ISMENA - Fie, Isabella, what an ill opinion you have of me?
But, Sister, 'tis much Alberto being so intimate
With Antonio, should never see you all this whole
Six Months of your being married.

CLARINA - Had you been bred any where
But in a Monastery, you would have known
'Tis not the custom here for Men to expose their
Wives to the view of any.

ISABELLA - I hear them coming, let's away,
And pray listen to the Truths I have already told you.
[They retire.

SCENE IV. The Same.

Enter Antonio and Alberto. Clarina and Ismena listen.

ALBERTO - Once more, Antonio, welcome back to Court.

ANTONIO - Oh my dear Friend, I long'd for thy Embraces;
How goes the Game I left with thee to play?
What says my Wife, my beautiful Clarina?

ALBERTO - Clarina!

ANTONIO - Yes, Clarina, have you not seen her yet?
I left the Court on purpose, for 'twas not handsome
For me to introduce you,
Lest she had look'd upon't as some design.

ALBERTO - Seen her – yes -

ANTONIO - And I conjur'd her too, to give you freedoms
Even equal to Antonio;
As far as I durst press with modesty,
And with pretence of Friendship;
And have you not attempted her?

ALBERTO - Yes, but 'tis in vain.

ANTONIO - Oh villanous Dissembler!   [Aside.

ALBERTO - She's cruel, strangely cruel,
And I'm resolv'd to give the Courtship o'er.

ANTONIO - Sure, Friend, thou hast not us'd thy wonted power.

ALBERTO - Yes, all that I know I'm master of, I us'd.

ANTONIO - But didst thou urge it home? did she not see
Thy Words and Actions did not well agree?
Canst thou dissemble well? didst cry and melt,
As if the pain you but express'd, you felt?
Didst kneel, and swear, and urge thy Quality,
Heightning it too with some Disgrace on me?
And didst thou too assail her feeble side?
For the best bait to Woman is her Pride;
Which some mis-call her Guard:
Didst thou present her with the set of Jewels?
For Women naturally are more inclin'd
To Avarice, than Men: pray tell me, Friend.
Vile Woman! did she take them -

ALBERTO - I never ask'd her that.

CLARINA - Poor Antonio, how I pity him.   [Aside.

ANTONIO - No!

ALBERTO - No, I've done enough to satisfy thy Jealousy.
Here, take your set of Jewels back again;   [Gives a Box.
Upon my Life Clarina is all Chastity.

ANTONIO - I were the happiest Man on Earth, were this but true;
But what are single Courtships? give her these,
Which will assist thy Tongue to win her Heart;
And that once got, the other soon will follow;
There's far more Women won by Gold than Industry:
Try that, my dear Alberto,
And save thy Eyes the trouble of dissembling.

ALBERTO - Content thee here, and do not tempt thy Fate,
I have regard unto thy Honour, Friend;
And should she yield, as Women are no Gods,
Where were thy future Joys?
What is't could make thee happy, or restore
That true Contentment which thou hadst before?
Alas! thou tempt'st me too, for I am frail,
And Love above my Friendship may prevail.

ANTONIO - This will not do;
No, as thou art my Friend, and lov'st my Honour,
Pursue Clarina further;
Rally afresh, and charge her with this Present,
Disturb her every night with Serenades;
Make Love-Songs to her, and then sing them too;
Thou hast a Voice enough alone to conquer.

ALBERTO - Fool, Antonio!   [Aside.

ANTONIO - Come, wilt thou undertake it once again?

ALBERTO - I would not.

ANTONIO - I am resolv'd to get this tryal made,
And if thou dost refuse thy Amity,
I'll try a Friend more willing, though less faithful;
With thee my Wife and Honour too are safe,
For should she yield, and I by that were lost,
'Twere yet some ease,
That none but thou wert witness to't.

ALBERTO - Well, if it must be done, I'ad rather do't,
Than you should be expos'd to th' scorn of others.

ANTONIO - Spoke like my noble Friend;
Come dine with her to day, for I must leave you,
And give you all the opportunity
A real Lover wishes with a Mistress.

ISMENA - So we have heard enough.

[Ex. Clarina and Ismena.

ANTONIO - Oh, were Clarina chaste, as on my Soul
I cannot doubt, more than that I believe
All Womankind may be seduc'd from Virtue;
I were the Man of all the World most bless'd
In such a Wife, and such a Friend as thou.

ALBERTO - But what if I prevail, Antonio?

ANTONIO - Then I'll renounce my faith in Womankind,
And place my satisfaction in thy Amity.
But see, she comes, I'll leave you to your task.

Enter Ismena and Isabella.

ISMENA - Antonio not yet gone
This must secure me.   [Pulls down her Veil.

ANTONIO - Clarina, why thus clouded?

ISABELLA - I see he has most happily mistaken.

ISMENA - I was going, Sir, to visit LAURA -

ANTONIO - You must not go, I've business to the Duke,

And you must entertain my Friend till my return;
It is a freedom not usual here amongst Ladies,
But I will have it so;
Whom I esteem, I'll have you do so too.

ISMENA - Sir, I am all obedience.

[Exit Antonio, she pulls off her Veil; Alberto salutes her with seeming lowness.

ALBERTO - Oh, how my Soul's divided
Between my Adoration and my Amity!   [Aside.
Friendship, thou sacred band, hold fast thy Interest;
For yonder Beauty has a subtle power,
And can undo that knot, which other Arts
Could ne'er invent a way for.

Enter Antonio, and listens at the Door.

ANTONIO - I'll see a little how he behaves himself.   [Aside.

ALBERTO - But she's Antonio's Wife; my Friend Antonio.   [Aside.
A Youth that made an Interest in my Soul,
When I had Language scarce to express my sense of it.

ANTONIO - Death! he speaks not to her.   [Aside.

ALBERTO - So grew we up to Man, and still more fixt;
And shall a gaudy Beauty,
A thing which t'other day I never saw,
Deprive my Heart of that kind Heat,
And place a new and unknown Fire within?   [Aside.
Clarina, 'tis unjust.

ISMENA - Sir, did you speak to me?

ALBERTO - I have betray'd my self   [Aside.
Madam, I was saying how unjust it was
Antonio should leave me alone with a Lady,
Being certainly the worst to entertain them in the World.

ANTONIO - His Face assures me he speaks of no Love to her now.

ISMENA - Alas, he speaks not to me.
Sure Isabella was mistaken, who told me that he lov'd me.
Alberto, if thou art oblig'd to me,   [Aside.
For what I have not yet observ'd in thee,
Oh, do not say my Heart was easily won,
But blame your Eyes, whose forces none can shun.

ANTONIO - Not a word, what can he mean by this?

ISMENA - Sir, will you please to sit a while?

ISABELLA - Madam, the inner Chamber is much better,
For there he may repose upon the Cushions
Till my Lord's return; I see he is not well
And you are both sick of one Disease.   [Aside.

ALBERTO - I thank you, here's more Air,
And that I need, for I am all on fire,   [Aside.
And every Look adds fuel to my flame.
I must avoid those Eyes, whose Light misguides me:
Madam, I have some business calls me hence,
And cannot wait my Friend's return.

ISMENA - Antonio, Sir, will think 'tis my neglect
That drove you hence; pray stay a little longer.

ALBERTO - You shall command me, if you can dispense
With so dull Company.

ISMENA - I can with any thing Antonio loves.

ALBERTO - Madam, it is a Virtue that becomes you;
For though your Husband should not merit this,
Your Goodness is not less to be admir'd;
But he's a Man so truly worth your Kindness,
That 'twere a Sin to doubt
Your Passion for him were not justly paid.

ISMENA - Sir, I believe you, and I hope he thinks
That my opinion of him equals yours;
'Tis plain he loves me not;   [Aside.
Perhaps his Virtue, thinking me Clarina,
May hide the real Passion of his Soul.
Oh Love, what dangerous Paths thou mak'st us tread!

ANTONIO - Cold, cold as Devotion, oh inhuman Friendship!   [Aside.

ALBERTO - What shall I do next? I must either be rude,
And say nothing, or speak of Love to her;
And then, my Friend, thou'rt lost should I prevail,
And I'm undone should she not hear my Tale,
Which for the World I would not have her hear;
And yet I fear my Eyes too much declare.

ISMENA - Since he's in so ill an Humour, let's leave him,
I'm satisfy'd now that thou'rt mistaken.

[Ex. Ismena and Isabella unseen.

ALBERTO - But they shall gaze no more on hers,

Nor stray beyond the limits of a just Salute.
I will my Honour to my Love prefer,
And my Antonio shall out-rival her.
[Looks about, and misses them.
Ah, am I left alone! how frail is Man!
That which last Moment I resolv'd upon,
I find my Heart already disapprove,
And grieve her loss; can this be ought but Love?
My Soul's dissatisfy'd now she is gone,
And yet but now I wish'd to be alone.
Inform me, Love, who shares the better part,
Friendship, or thee, in my divided Heart.   [Offers to go.

Enter Antonio, and stays him.

ANTONIO - Whither in such haste?
Thou look'st e'en as sad as a Lover repuls'd,
I fear that Fate's not thine.

ALBERTO - Now for a lye to satisfy him.   [Aside.
Prithee discharge me of this toil of dissembling,
Of which I grow as weary as she's of hearing it.

ANTONIO - Indeed!

ALBERTO - Sure thou hast a design to make her hate me.

ANTONIO - Do you think so in earnest, why, was she angry?

ALBERTO - Oh! hadst thou seen her pretty blushing Scorn,
Which she would fain have hid,
Thou wouldst have pitied what I made her suffer.

ANTONIO - Is't possible!
And didst present her with the Box of Jewels?

ALBERTO - Yes.

ANTONIO - And kneel, and cry and swear, and -

ALBERTO - All, all.

ANTONIO - I hardly gave thee time for so much Courtship,
But you are sure she was displeased with it?

ALBERTO - Extremely.

ANTONIO - Enough, Alberto; adieu to thee and Friendship.

ALBERTO - What mean you?

ANTONIO - Ask your own Guilt, it will inform thee best.

ALBERTO - Thou canst not think Clarina has abus'd thee.

ANTONIO - I do not think she has, nor have you try'd her;
In that you have not only disoblig'd me,
But now you would impose upon my Weakness
Did I not see how unconcern'd you were,
And hardly paying her a due respect;
And when she even invited thee to speak,
Most rudely thou wert silent?

ALBERTO - Be calm, Antonio, I confess my error,
And hate that Virtue taught me to deceive thee;
Here, take my Hand,
I'll serve you in good earnest.

ANTONIO - And now I do believe thee,
Go, thou shalt lose no time, I must away,
My Soul's in torment, till I am confirm'd
Of my Clarina's Virtue;
I do believe thou hast a generous Shame,
For what thou'st said and done to me thy Friend.
For could I doubt thy Love, oh, how ridiculous
This act of mine would seem!
But 'tis to thee, as to my Soul I come,
Disputing every petty Crime and Doubt.

ALBERTO - Antonio, if there need an Oath between us

ANTONIO - No, I credit thee; go in,
And prithee dress thy Eyes in all their Charms;
For this uncertainty disturbs me more,
Than if I knew Clarina were a - Whore.

[Exeunt severally.

ACT II.

SCENE I. The Apartment of Frederick.

Enter Frederick with a Letter, and Galliard.

FREDERICK - Not allow me to speak to her, say ye, 'tis strange;
Didst say it was the Prince that sent thee?

GALLIARD - My Lord, I did, but he says, he cares not for
A thousand Princes.

FREDERICK - I am resolv'd I will see this Woman;
Harkye, go back again and say -   [Whispers.

Enter Lorenzo drunk.

LORENZO - Hah, the Prince, he must not see me
In this pickle; for I would not lose my Reputation
Of Wenching for this of Drinking;
And I am sure I cannot be excellent at both,
They are inconsistent.

GALLIARD - I shall, my Lord.   [Exit.

LORENZO - Your Highness's humble Servant.

FREDERICK - Ha, ha, what, Lorenzo in debauch?

LORENZO - Now my Tongue will betray me:
Faith, my Lord, I have took six, but am come briskly off;
By this hand, my Lord, I am Cock over five
Stout Rogues too, I can tell you, at this sport.

FREDERICK - I did not think thou hadst had that Virtue.

LORENZO - I'll tell you, Sir, 'tis necessary those of my
Office and Quality should have more Virtues
Than one to recommend them;
But to tell you truth, for now I am most apt for that,
I was drunk in mere Malice to day.

FREDERICK - Malice, against whom, prithee?

LORENZO - Why, why, Sir, the humorous old Fellow,
My Father,
He will not hear reason from me when I am sober.
My Lord, you know Curtius is an honest Fellow,
And one of us too;
My Sister Laura is a good pretty Wench,
He loves her, and she likes him;
And because this testy old Blade has done himself,
Do you think I can bring him to consider?
No, not for my Life, he won't consider, Sir;
And now am I got drunk to see how that will edify him.

FREDERICK - How! is Laura, the Mistress of Curtius, your Sister?

LORENZO - Yes, marry is she, Sir, at least by the Mother's side;
And to tell you truth,
We are too good-natur'd to believe
Salvator our Father.

FREDERICK - Thy Sister, and Daughter to Salvator?

LORENZO - So said my Mother, but she was handsome;
And on my conscience liv'd e'en in such another
Debauch'd World as 'tis now, let them say
What they will of their primitive Virtue.

FREDERICK - May not I see this Sister of thine, Lorenzo?

LORENZO - Yes, by Venus, shall you, Sir,
An she were my Mother.

FREDERICK - But art sure thy Father will permit us?

LORENZO - My Father permit us!
He may do what he will when I am sober,
But being thus fortify'd with potent Wine,
He must yield obedience to my Will.
Why, my Lord, I'll tell you,
I'll make him ask me blessing when I am in this
Almighty Power.

FREDERICK - And is thy Sister so very fine?

LORENZO - The Girl is well, and if she were not my Sister,
I would give you a more certain Proof of my
Opinion of her;
She has excellent good Hair, fine Teeth,
And good Hands, and the best natur'd Fool
Come, come, Sir, I'll bring you to her,
And then I'll leave you;
For I have a small Affair of Love to dispatch.

FREDERICK - This is a freedom that sutes not with the
Humour of an Italian.

LORENZO - No, faith, my Lord; I believe my Mother play'd
Foul play with some Englishman;
I am so willing to do you a good office to my Sister.
And if by her Humour you become of that opinion too,
I shall hope to render myself more acceptable
To you by that Franchise.

Enter Galliard, whispers.

FREDERICK - Thou knowest my grateful Temper,
No matter; here, carry this Letter to Cloris,
And make some excuse for my not coming this Evening.
[Gives him a Letter, and goes out with Lorenzo.

GALLIARD - So, poor Lass, 'tis a hundred to one if she be not

Lay'd by now, and Laura must succeed her:
Well, even Frederick, I see, is but a Man,
But his Youth and Quality will excuse him;
And 'twill be call'd Gallantry in him,
When in one of us, 'tis Ill-nature and Inconstancy.   [Exit.

SCENE II. Antonio's House.

Enter Ismena and Isabella.

ISABELLA - Nay, Madam, 'tis in vain to deny it;
Do you think I have liv'd to these years,
And cannot interpret cross Arms, imperfect Replies,
Your sudden Weepings, your often Sighing,
Your melancholy Walks, and making Verses too?
And yet I must not say that this is Love.

ISMENA - Art thou so notable a Judge of it?

ISABELLA - I should be, or I am a very dull Scholar,
For I have lost the foolish Boy as many Darts,
As any Woman of my age in Florence.

ISMENA - Thou hast paid dear for thy knowledge then.

ISABELLA - No, the hurt ones did, the other still made good, with verylittle
Pain on either side.

ISMENA - I must confess, I think it is not so hard to get
Wounds, as 'tis to get them cur'd again.

ISABELLA - I am not of your opinion, nor ever saw that
Man who had not Faults to Cure,
As well as Charms to kill.

ISMENA - Since thou'rt so good a Judge of Men,
Prithee tell me how thou lik'st Alberto.

ISABELLA - I knew 'twould come to this   [Aside.
Why, well, Madam.

ISMENA - No more than so?

ISABELLA - Yes, wondrous well, since I am sure he loves you,
And that indeed raises a Man's Value.

ISMENA - Thou art deceiv'd, I do not think he loves me.

ISABELLA - Madam, you cannot but see a thousand Marks on't.

ISMENA - Thou hast more Skill than I;
But prithee why does he not tell me so himself?

ISABELLA - Oh Madam, whilst he takes you for Clarina,
'Twould shew his disrespect to tell his Love?
But when he knows Ismena is the Object,
He'll tire you with the wish'd for story.

ISMENA - Ah, thou art a pleasing Flatterer.

Enter Page.

PAGE - Madam, Alberto is without.

ISMENA - Tell him I'm indispos'd, and cannot see him now.

ISABELLA - Nay, good Madam, see him now by all means,
For I am sure my Lord Antonio is absent on purpose.
Bid him come in, Boy.   [Exit Page.

Enter Alberto.

ISMENA - Antonio, Sir, is not return'd.

ALBERTO - Madam, this Visit was not meant to him,
But by a Cause more pressing I am brought,
Such as my Passion, not My Friendship taught;
A Passion which my Sighs have only shewn,
And now beg leave my bashful Tongue may own.
The knowledge, Madam, will not much surprise,
Which you have gain'd already from mine Eyes;
My timorous Heart that way my Tongue would spare,
And tells you of the Flames you've kindled there:
'Tis long I've suffered under this Constraint,
Have always suffer'd, but ne'er made Complaint;
And now against my will I must reveal
What Love and my Respect would fain conceal.

ISMENA - What mean you, Sir? what have you seen in me,
That should encourage this temerity?

ALBERTO - A world of Beauties, and a world of Charms,
And every Smile and Frown begets new harms;
In vain I strove my Passion to subdue,
Which still increas'd the more I look'd on you;
Nor will my Heart permit me to retire,
But makes my Eyes the convoys to my Fire,
And not one Glance you send is cast away.

ISMENA - Enough, my Lord, have you nought else to say?
The Plot's betray'd, and can no further go;   [Smiles.

The Stratagem's discover'd to the Foe;
I find Antonio has more Love than Wit,
And I'll endeavour too to merit it.

ALBERTO - What you have said, I do confess is true,
Antonio beg'd I would make love to you;
But, Madam, whilst my heart was unconfin'd,
A thousand ways the Treachery I declin'd
But now, Clarina, by my Life I swear,
It is my own concern that brings me here:
Had he been just to you, I had suppress'd
The Flames your Eyes have kindled in my Breast;
But his Suspicion rais'd my Passion more,
And his Injustice taught me to adore:
But 'tis a Passion which you may allow,
Since its effects shall never injure you.

ISMENA - You have oblig'd me, Sir, by your Confession,
And I shall own it too at such a rate,
As both becomes my Duty to Antonio,
And my Respect to you; but I must beg
You'll never name your Passion to me more,
That guilty Language, Sir, I must not hear:
And yet your silence kills me.   [Aside.

ISABELLA - Very well dissembled.   [Aside.

ALBERTO - I can obey you, Madam, though I cannot live,
Whilst you command me silence;
For 'tis a Flame that dares not look abroad
To seek for pity from another's Eyes.

ISMENA - How he moves me! if this were real now,
Or that he knew to whom he made this Courtship -   [Aside.

ALBERTO - Oh, do not turn away as if displeas'd.

ISMENA - No more, you've discompos'd my thoughts;
Be gone, and never let me see thy Face again.

ALBERTO - Madam, I go, and will no more offend you,
But I will look my last - farewel.   [Offers to go.

ISABELLA - Pray, Madam, call him back, he may be desperate.
My Lord, return -

ISMENA - Alberto, tell me what you'd have me do.

ALBERTO - Ah, Madam, do not put me to my choice,
For Lovers are unreasonable;
If I might name it, I would have you love me.

ISMENA - Love you, and what would be the end of that?

ALBERTO - I cannot tell, but wish you were inclin'd
To make a tryal, Madam;
I have no thought or wish beyond that Blessing,
And that once gain'd, sure I should ask no more.

ISMENA - Were I inclin'd to this, have you consider'd
The fatal Consequences which attend
The breach of Vows and Friendship?

ALBERTO - Madam, Antonio first was false to you,
And not to punish that were such a Virtue
As he would never thank you for;
By all that's good, till he prov'd so to you,
He had my Soul in keeping;
But this act makes me resolve
To recompense his Folly.

ISMENA - You've found the easiest Passage to my Heart,
You've took it on the weakest side;
But I must beg you will pretend no further.

ALBERTO - Divine Clarina, let me pay my thanks
In this submissive Posture, and never rise,   [Kneels.
Till I can gain so much upon your Credit,
As to believe my Passion tends no farther
Than to adore you thus and thus possess you.
[Kisses her hand, and bows.

ISMENA - Have not I dissembled finely, Isabella?   [Aside.

ISABELLA - Yes, if you could make me believe 'tis so.   [Aside.

ISMENA - Rise, Sir, and leave me, that I may blush alone
For what I've parted with so easily;
Pray do not visit me again too soon,
But use your own discretion, and be secret.

ALBERTO - Madam, the blessed Secret here is lodg'd,
Which Time shall ne'er reveal to human Knowledge.   [Ex. Alberto.

ISMENA - I'm glad he's gone before Antonio's return.

Enter Laura weeping.

What, Laura, all in Tears! the reason, pray.

LAURA - Madam, the Prince, conducted by my Brother,
About an Hour since made me a Visit;

The Man of all the World I would have shun'd,
Knowing his amorous and inconstant Temper.
At his approach he blusht and started back,
And I with great amazement did the like.
With fear I lost all power of going from him.
As he had done of making his Address;
He gaz'd and wonder'd, and I gaz'd on him,
And from his silence I became amaz'd.
My Brother stood confounded at our Postures,
And only by the motion of his Head
(Which now he turn'd to me, then on the Prince)
We knew that he had Life.

ISMENA - Well, how recover'd ye?

LAURA - The Prince then kneel'd, but could approach no nearer;
And then as if he'd taken me for some Deity,
He made a long disorder'd amorous Speech,
Which brought me back to Sense again:
But Lorenzo told him that I was a Mortal,
And brought him nearer to me,
Where he began to make such Vows of Love

ISMENA - What then?

LAURA - Then I am ruin'd
To all I said he found a contradiction,
And my denials did but more inflame him;
I told him of the Vows I'ad made to Curtius,
But he reply'd that Curtius was a Subject.
But sure at last I'd won upon his Goodness,
Had not my Father enter'd,
To whom the Prince addrest himself;
And with his moving tale so won upon him,
Or rather by his Quality,
That he has gain'd his leave to visit me,
And quite forbids me e'er to speak to Curtius.

ISMENA - Alas the day, is this all?

LAURA - All! can there be more to make me miserable?

ISMENA - I see no reason thou hast to complain:
Come, wipe your Eyes, and take a good Heart;
For I'll tell thee a Story of my own,
That will let thee see I have much more cause to weep;
And yet I have a thousand little Stratagems
In my Head, which give me as many hopes:
This unlucky restraint upon our Sex,
Makes us all cunning; and that shall assist thee now
With my help, I warrant thee;

Come in with me, and know the rest.

[Exeunt.

ISABELLA - So, so, disguise it how you will,
I know you are a real Lover;
And that secret shall advance my Love-design.
Yes, Madam, now I will be serv'd by you,
Or you shall fail to find a Friend of me.   [Ex. ISABELLA -

SCENE III. The Street.

Enter Lorenzo drunk, with a Page, and Musick, as in the dark.

LORENZO - Here's the Door, begin and play your best,
But let them be soft low Notes, do you hear?   [They play.

Enter Antonio.

ANTONIO - Musick at my Lodgings! it is Alberto;
Oh, how I love him for't, if Clarina stand his
Courtship, I am made;
I languish between Hope and Fear.

LORENZO - Stay, Friend, I hear somebody.   [Musick ceases.

PAGE - 'Tis nobody, Sir.

Enter Isabella.

ISABELLA - 'Tis Lorenzo, and my Plot's ripe;   [Aside.
[Lorenzo being retir'd the while a little further.

'Twill not sure be hard to get him, under pretence
Of seeing Clarina, into my Chamber,
And then I'll order him at my pleasure;
Ismena is on my side, for I know all her Secrets,
And she must wink at mine therefore.   [She retires.

LORENZO - Thou art in the right, Boy,
I think indeed 'twas nothing.   [Plays again.

Enter Alberto.

ALBERTO - She yields, bad Woman!
Why so easily won?
By me too, who am thy Husband's Friend:
Oh dangerous Boldness! unconsidering Woman!
I lov'd thee, whilst I thought thou couldst not yield;
But now that Easiness has undone thy Interest in my Heart,

I'll back, and tell thee that it was to try thee.

LORENZO - No, no, 'twas my Fears, away with the Song,
I'll take it on your word that 'tis fit for my purpose.

FIDDLER - I'll warrant you, my Lord.

SONG
In vain I have labour'd the Victor to prove
Of a Heart that can ne'er give attendance to Love;
So hard to be done.
That nothing so young
Could e'er have resisted a Passion so long.

Yet nothing I left unattempted or said,
That might soften the Heart of this pitiless Maid;
But still she was shy,
And would blushing deny,
Whilst her willinger Eyes gave her Language the lye.

Since, Phillis, my Passion you vow to despise,
Withdraw the false Hopes from your flattering Eyes:
For whilst they inspire
A resistless vain Fire,
We shall grow to abhor, what we now do admire.   [Ex. Musick.

ALBERTO - What's this, and at Clarina's Lodgings too?
Sure 'tis Antonio, impatient of delay,
Gives her a Serenade for me.

Enter Isabella.

ISABELLA - 'Tis the Fool himself
My Lord, where are you?

ALBERTO - How! a Woman's Voice! 'tis dark, I'll advance.

LORENZO - Thou Simpleton, I told thee there was somebody.

PAGE - Lord, Sir, 'tis only Isabella that calls you.

LORENZO - Away, Sirrah, I find by my fears 'tis no Woman.
[Goes out with the Page.

ISABELLA - Why don't you come? here's nobody.

ALBERTO - Here I am.

ISABELLA - Where?

ALBERTO - Here.   [Gives her his Hand.

ISABELLA - My Lord, you may venture, Clarina will be
Alone within this Hour, where you shall entertain
Her at your freedom: but you must stay awhile in my
Chamber till my Lord's a bed;
For none but I must know of the favour she designs you.

ALBERTO - Oh Gods! what Language do I hear
False and Perfidious Woman, I might have thought,
Since thou wert gain'd so easily by me,
Thou wouldst with equal haste yield to another.

ISABELLA - It is not Lorenzo, what shall I do?   [She steals in.

Enter Lorenzo and Page.

LORENZO - A Pox of all damn'd cowardly fear!
Now did I think I had drunk Nature up to Resolution:
I have heard of those that could have dar'd in their Drink;
But I find, drunk or sober, 'tis all one in me.

ALBERTO - The Traitor's here,
Whom I will kill whoe'er he be.

LORENZO - Boy, go see for Isabella.

PAGE - I see a Man should not be a Coward and a Lover
At once - Isabella, Isabella, she's gone, Sir.   [Calls.

ALBERTO - Yes, Villain, she's gone, and in her room
Is one that will chastise thy Boldness.

LORENZO - That's a proud word though, whoe'er thou be;
But how I shall avoid it, is past my Understanding.

ALBERTO - Where art thou, Slave?
[Alberto gropes for him, he avoids him.

PAGE - Take heart, Sir, here's company which I will
Get to assist you -

Enter Antonio.

Sir, as you are a Gentleman, assist a stranger set upon by Thieves.

[They fight, Antonio with Alberto, Alberto falls, is wounded. Lorenzo and Page run away the while.

ALBERTO - Whoe'er thou be'st that takes the Traitor's part,
Commend me to the wrong'd Antonio.

ANTONIO - Alberto! dear Alberto, is it thee?

ALBERTO - Antonio!

ANTONIO - I am asham'd to say I am Antonio;
Oh Gods, why would you suffer this mistake?

ALBERTO - I am not wounded much,
My greatest pain is my concern for thee;
Friend, thou art wrong'd, falsely and basely wrong'd;
Clarina, whom you lov'd and fear'd,
Has now betray'd thy Honour with her own.

ANTONIO - Without that sad addition to my Grief,
I should not long have born the weight of Life,
Having destroy'd thine by a dire mistake.

ALBERTO - Thou art deceiv'd.

ANTONIO - Alas, why was it not permitted me
To lose my Friend, or Wife? had one surviv'd,
I might have dy'd in silence for the other;
Oh my Alberto! oh Clarina too!   [Weeps.

ALBERTO - Come, do not grieve for me, I shall be well,
I yet find strength enough to get away;
And then I'll let thee know my Fate and thine.

[Exeunt.

SCENE IV. Antonio's House.

Enter Clarina, Ismena, and Isabella weeping.

ISABELLA - For Heaven sake, Madam, pardon me.

CLARINA - Be dumb for ever, false and treacherous Woman,
Was there no way but this to mask your Cheat?
A Lye which has undone us all.

ISABELLA - Alas, 'twas in the dark, how could I know him?
Pray forgive it me, and try my future Service.

CLARINA - I never will forgive thee, naughty Girl;
Alberto now incens'd will tell Antonio all.

ISABELLA - What need you care, Madam?
You are secure enough.

CLARINA - Thou salv'st an Error with a greater still;
Dost thou not know Antonio's Jealousy,

Which yet is moderate, rais'd to a higher pitch,
May ruin me, Ismena, and thy self?

ISMENA - Sister, there cannot be much harm in this;
'Tis an ill chance, 'tis true, for by it we have lost
The pleasure of an innocent Revenge
Upon Antonio; but if understood,
We have but miss'd that end.

CLARINA - Oh Ismena!
This Jealousy is an unapprehensive madness,
A non-sense which does still abandon Reason.

ISABELLA - Madam, early in the Morning
I'll to Alberto's Lodgings, and tell him the mistake.

CLARINA - 'Twill be too late.

ISMENA - Sister, what think you if I go myself?

CLARINA - You should not be so daring;
Besides, I blush to think what strange opinion
He'll entertain of me the while.

ISMENA - Do not let that afflict you.
Fetch my Veil, and if Antonio chance to ask for me,
Tell him I'm gone to Laura.   [Ex. ISABELLA -
Believe me, I will set all strait again.

Enter Isabella with the Veil.

CLARINA - Thou hast more Courage, Girl, than I.

ISMENA - What need is there of much of that,
To encounter a gay young Lover,
Where I am sure there cannot be much danger?

CLARINA - Well, take your chance, I wish you luck, Sir,
For I am e'en as much bent upon Revenge,
As thou art upon Marriage.

ISMENA - Come, my Veil, this and the Night
Will enough secure me.   [Puts on the Veil and goes out.

[Ex. Clarina and Isabella.

SCENE V. A Chamber in Alberto's House.

Discovers Alberto and Antonio.

ALBERTO - Nay, thou shalt see't before thou dost revenge it;
In such a case, thy self should be the Witness,
She knows not what has past to night between us,
Nor should she, if thou couldst contain thy Rage;
And that, Antonio, you shall promise me:
To morrow place thy self behind the Arras,
And from thy Eyes thy own Misfortunes know.
What will not disobliged Passion do?   [Aside.

ANTONIO - I'll hide my Anger in a seeming calm,
And what I have to do consult the while,
And mask my Vengeance underneath a Smile.   [Ex. ANTONIO -

Enter Page.

PAGE - My Lord, there is without a Lady
Desires to speak with you.

ALBERTO - Who is't?

PAGE - I know not, Sir, she's veiled.   [Exit Page.

Enter Ismena weeping.

ALBERTO - Conduct her in.

ISMENA - Oh Alberto, Isabella has undone us all!

ALBERTO - She weeps, and looks as innocent!
What mean you, false dissembling Clarina?
What, have you borrow'd from Deceit new Charms,
And think'st to fool me to a new belief?

ISMENA - How, Sir, can you too be unkind?
Nay then 'tis time to die; alas, there wanted but your credit
To this mistake, to make me truly miserable.

ALBERTO - What Credit? What Mistake? oh, undeceive me,
For I have done thee Injuries past Forgiveness,
If thou be'st truly innocent.

ISMENA - If Isabella, under pretence of courting me
For Lorenzo, whom she designs to
Make a Husband,
Has given him freedoms will undo my Honour,
If not prevented soon.

ALBERTO - May I credit this, and that it was not by thy
Command she did it?

ISMENA - Be witness, Heaven, my Innocence in this,

Which if you will believe, I'm safe again.

ALBERTO - I do believe thee, but thou art not safe,
Here, take this Poyniard, and revenge thy Wrongs,
Wrongs which I dare not beg a Pardon for.   [He gives her a Dagger.

ISMENA - Why, Sir, what have you done? have you
Deceiv'd me, and do you not indeed love me?

ALBERTO - Oh Clarina! do not ask that Question,
Too much of that has made me ruin thee;
It made me jealous, drunk with Jealousy,
And then I did unravel all my Secrets.

ISMENA - What Secrets, Sir? you have then seen Antonio.

ALBERTO - Yes.

Ismena – Hah. Now, Wit, if e'er thou did'st possess
A Woman, assist her at her need.   [Aside.
Well, Sir, rise and tell me all.

ALBERTO - I will not rise till you have pardoned me,
Or punished my Misfortune.

ISMENA - Be what it will, I do forgive it thee.

ALBERTO - Antonio, Madam, knows my Happiness,
For in my Rage I told him that you lov'd me;
What shall I do?

ISMENA - I cannot blame you though it were unkind.

ALBERTO - This I could help, but I have promis'd him,
That he shall be a witness of this Truth;
What say you, Madam, do I not merit Death?
Oh speak, and let me know my doom whate'er it be.

ISMENA - Make good your Word.

ALBERTO - What mean you?

ISMENA - What you have promised him, perform as you intended.

ALBERTO - What then?

ISMENA - Then come as you design'd to visit me.

ALBERTO - But let me know what 'tis you mean to do,
That I may act accordingly.

ISMENA - No. Answer me to every Question ask'd,
And I perhaps may set all strait again;
It is now late, and I must not be missing:
But if you love me, be no more jealous of me,
Farewel.

ALBERTO - Must I be ignorant then of your Design?

ISMENA - Yes, Alberto;
And you shall see what Love will make a Woman do.
[He leads her out.

ALBERTO - Now am I caught again, inconstant Nature.
Would she had less of Beauty or of Wit,
Or that Antonio did but less deserve her;
Or that she were not married,
Or I'ad less Virtue, for 'tis that which awes me.
That tender sense of nothing,
And makes the other Reasons seem as Bugbears.
I love Clarina more than he can do.
And yet this Virtue doth oppose that Love,
Tells me there lurks a Treason there
Against Antonio's and Clarina's Virtue.
'Tis but too true indeed, and I'm not safe,
Whilst I conceal the Criminal within:
I must reveal it, for whilst I hide the Traitor,
I seem to love the Treason too;
I will resign it then, since 'tis less blame
To perish by my Pain, than live with Shame.   [Exit.

ACT III.

SCENE I. A Room in Salvator's House.

Enter Frederick and Laura.

FREDERICK - Laura, consider well my Quality,
And be not angry with your Father's Confidence,
Who left us here alone.

LAURA - He will repent that Freedom when he knows
What use you've made on't, Sir.

FREDERICK - Fy, fy, Laura, a Lady bred at Court, and
Yet want complaisance enough to entertain
A Gallant in private! this coy Humour
Is not à-la-mode. Be not so peevish with a Heart that dies for you.

LAURA - Pray tell me, Sir, what is't in me that can

Encourage this?

FREDERICK - That which is in all lovely Women, Laura;
A thousand Blushes play about your Cheeks,
Which shows the briskness of the Blood that warms them.
If I but tell you how I do adore you,
You strait decline your Eyes;
Which does declare you understand my meaning,
And every Smile or Frown betrays your thoughts,
And yet you cry, you do not give me cause.

Enter Maid.

Maid. Curtius, Madam, waits without.

FREDERICK - I do not like his haste,
Tell him he cannot be admitted now.

LAURA - Sir, he is one that merits better treatment from you;
How can you injure thus the Man you love?

FREDERICK - Oh Madam, ask your Eyes, those powerful Attracts.
And do not call their Forces so in question,
As to believe they kindle feeble Fires,
Such as a Friendship can surmount. No, Laura,
They've done far greater Miracles.

LAURA - Sir, 'tis in vain you tell me of their Power,
Unless they could have made a nobler Conquest
Than Hearts that yield to every petty Victor.
Look on me well,
Can nothing here inform you of my Soul,
And how it scorns to treat on these Conditions?
[Looks on him, he gazes with a half Smile.

FREDERICK - Faith, no, Laura.
I see nothing there but wondrous Beauty,
And a deal of needless Pride and Scorn,
And such as may be humbled.

LAURA - Sir, you mistake, that never can abate.
But yet I know your Power may do me injuries;
But I believe you're guilty of no Sin,
Save your Inconstancy, which is sufficient;
And, Sir, I beg I may not be the first   [Kneels and weeps.
May find new Crimes about you.

FREDERICK - Rise, Laura, thou hast but too many Beauties,
Which pray be careful that you keep conceal'd.   [Offers to go.

LAURA - I humbly thank you, Sir.

FREDERICK - But why should this interposing Virtue check me?
Stay, Laura, tell me; must you marry Curtius?

LAURA - Yes, Sir, I must.

FREDERICK - Laura, you must not.

LAURA - How, Sir!

FREDERICK - I say you shall not marry him,
Unless you offer up a Victim,
That may appease the Anger you have rais'd in me.

LAURA - I'll offer up a thousand Prayers and Tears.

FREDERICK - That will not do.
Since thou'st deny'd my just Pretensions to thee,
No less than what I told you of shall satisfy me.

LAURA - Oh, where is all your Honour and your Virtue?

FREDERICK - Just where it was, there's no such real thing.
I know that thou wert made to be possest,
And he that does refuse it, loves thee least.
There's danger in my Love, and your Delay,
And you are most secure whilst you obey.   [He pulls her gently.

LAURA - Then this shall be my safety, hold off,   [She draws a Dagger.
Or I'll forget you are my Prince.   [He laughs.

FREDERICK - Pretty Virago, how you raise my Love?
I have a Dagger too; what will you do?   [Shows her a Dagger.

Enter Curtius.

CURTIUS - How! the Prince! arm'd against Laura too!   [Draws.

FREDERICK - Traitor, dost draw upon thy Prince?

CURTIUS - Your Pardon, Sir, I meant it on a Ravisher,
A foul misguided Villain,   [Bows.
One that scarce merits the brave name of Man;
One that betrays his Friend, forsakes his Wife,
And would commit a Rape upon my Mistress.

FREDERICK - Her Presence is thy Safety, be gone and leave me.

CURTIUS - By no means, Sir; the Villain may return,
To which fair Laura, should not be expos'd.

FREDERICK - Slave, dar'st thou disobey?   [Offers to fight.

CURTIUS - Hold, Sir, and do not make me guilty of a Sin,
Greater than that of yours.

Enter Salvator.

SALVATOR - Gods pity me; here's fine doings! Why, how
Came this roistring Youngster into my House? Sir,
Who sent for you, hah?

CURTIUS - Love.

SALVATOR - Love, with a Witness to whom? my Daughter?
No, Sir, she's otherwise dispos'd of I can assure
You. Be gone and leave my House, and that quickly
Too; and thank me that I do not secure
Thee for a Traitor.

CURTIUS - Will you not hear me speak?

SALVATOR - Not a word, Sir, go, be gone; unless your
Highness will have him apprehended.   [To FREDERICK -

FREDERICK - No, Sir, it shall not need - Curtius, look
To hear from me.
[Comes up to him, and tells him so in a menacing Tone, and go out severally.

SALVATOR - Go, Mrs. Minks, get you in.

[Ex. Salvator and LAURA -

SCENE II. A Street.

Enter Frederick passing in Anger over the Stage, meets Lorenzo.

LORENZO - O Sir, I'm glad I've found you; for
I have the rarest News for you.

FREDERICK - What News?

LORENZO - Oh the Devil, he's angry; Why, Sir, the prettiest young -

FREDERICK - There's for your Intelligence.   [Strikes him, and goes out.

LORENZO - So, very well; how mortal is the favour of
Princes! these be turns of State now; what the
Devil ails he trow; sure he could not be
Offended with the News I have brought him;
If he be, he's strangely out of tune:

And sure he has too much Wit to grow virtuous at these
Years. No, no, he has had some repulse from a
Lady; and that's a wonder; for he has a Tongue and a
Purse that seldom fails: if Youth and Vigour would
Stretch as far, he were the wonder of the Age.

Enter Curtius.

CURTIUS - Lorenzo, didst thou see the Prince?

LORENZO - Marry, did I, and feel him too.

CURTIUS - Why, did he strike you?

LORENZO - I'm no true Subject if he did not; and that
Only for doing that Service which once was most acceptable
To him. Prithee what's the matter with him, hah?

CURTIUS - I know not, leave me.

LORENZO - Leave thee, what, art thou out of humour too?
Let me but know who 'tis has disoblig'd thee, and I'll -

CURTIUS - What wilt thou?

LORENZO - Never see his Face more, if a Man.

CURTIUS - And what if a Woman?

LORENZO - Then she's an idle peevish Slut, I'll warrant her.

CURTIUS - Conclude it so, and leave me.

LORENZO - Nay, now thou hast said the only thing that could
Keep me with thee, thou mayst be desperate; I'll
Tell you, Curtius, these female Mischiefs make Men
Take dangerous Resolutions sometimes.

Enter Alberto.

ALBERTO - Curtius, I've something to deliver to your Ear.
[Whispers.

CURTIUS - Any thing from Alberto is welcome.

LORENZO - Well, I will be hang'd if there be not some
Mischief in agitation; it cannot be wenching;
They look all too dull and sober for that;
And besides, then I should have been a party concern'd.

CURTIUS - The place and time.

ALBERTO - An hour hence i'th' Grove by the River-side.

CURTIUS - Alone, thou say'st?

ALBERTO - Alone, the Prince will have it so.

CURTIUS - I will not fail a moment.   [Ex. Alberto.
So this has eas'd my heart of half its Load.

LORENZO - I'll sneak away, for this is some fighting
Business, and I may perhaps be invited a Second,
A Compliment I care not for.   [Offers to go.

CURTIUS - Lorenzo, a word with you.

LORENZO - 'Tis so, what shall I do now?   [Aside.

CURTIUS - Stay.

LORENZO - I am a little in haste, my Lord.

CURTIUS - I shall soon dispatch you.

LORENZO - I believe so, for I am half dead already
With Fear. [Aside.] Sir, I have promis'd to make a visit
To a Lady, and -

CURTIUS - What I've to say will not detain you long.

LORENZO - What a Dog was I, I went not
When he first desir'd me to go!
Oh Impertinency, thou art justly rewarded!

CURTIUS - Lorenzo, may I believe you love me?

LORENZO - Now what shall I say, Ay or no?   [Aside.
The Devil take me if I know.

CURTIUS - Will you do me a favour?

LORENZO - There 'tis again.   [Aside.

CURTIUS - I know I may trust thee with a secret.

LORENZO - Truly, Curtius, I cannot tell.
In some cases I am not very retentive.

CURTIUS - I am going about a business, that perhaps
May take up all the time I have to live,
And I may never see thy Sister more;

Will you oblige me in a Message to her?

LORENZO - You know you may command me;
I'm glad 'tis no worse.   [Aside.

CURTIUS - Come, go with me into my Cabinet,
And there I'll write to Laura;
And prithee if thou hear'st that I am dead,
Tell her I fell a Sacrifice to her,
And that's enough, she understands the rest.

LORENZO - But harkye, Curtius, by your favour, this is but a
Scurvy Tale to carry to your Mistress;
I hope you are not in earnest.

CURTIUS - Yes.

LORENZO - Yes! why, what a foolish idle humour's this in you?
I vow 'twill go near to break the poor Girl's Heart;
Come, be advis'd, Man.

CURTIUS - Perhaps I may consider on't for that reason.

LORENZO - There are few that go about such businesses,
But have one thing or other to consider in favour of Life;
I find that even in the most magnanimous:
Prithee who is't with?

CURTIUS - That's counsel: and pray let this too which I have
Told you be a Secret, for 'twill concern your Life.

LORENZO - Good Curtius, take it back again then;
For a hundred to one but my over-care of keeping it
Will betray it.

CURTIUS - Thou lovest thy self better.

LORENZO - Well, that's a comfort yet.

[Exeunt.

SCENE III. A Wood.

Enter Cloris dressed like a Country-Boy, follow'd by Guilliam a Clown; Cloris comes reading a Letter.

CLORIS - [Reads.] Cloris, beware of Men; for though I my self be one,
Yet I have the Frailties of my Sex, and can dissemble too;
Trust none of us, for if thou dost, thou art undone;
We make Vows to all alike we see,
And even the best of Men, the Prince,

Is not to be credited in an affair of Love.
Oh Curtius, thy advice was very kind;
Had it arriv'd before I'ad been undone!
Can Frederick too be false!
A Prince, and be unjust to her that loves him too?
Surely it is impossible
Perhaps thou lov'st me too, and this may be
[Pointing to the Letter.
Some Plot of thine to try my Constancy:
Howe'er it be, since he could fail last night
Of seeing me, I have at least a cause to justify
This shameful change; and sure in this Disguise,
I shall not soon be known, dost think I shall?   [Looks on herself.

GUILLIAM - Why, forsooth, what do you intend to pass for,
A Maid or a Boy?

CLORIS - Why, what I seem to be, will it not do?

GUILLIAM - Yes, yes, it may do, but I know not what;
I would Love would transmography me to a Maid now,
We should be the prettiest Couple:
Don't you remember when you dress'd me up the last
Carnival, was I not the woundiest handsome Lass
A body could see in a Summer's day?
There was Claud the Shepherd as freakish after me,
I'll warrant you, and simper'd and tript it like any thing.

CLORIS - Ay, but they say 'tis dangerous for young
Maids to live at Court.

GUILLIAM - Nay, then I should be loth to give temptation.
Pray, forsooth, what's that you read so often there?

CLORIS - An advice to young Maids that are in love.

GUILLIAM - Ay, ay, that same Love is a very vengeance thing,
Wou'd I were in love too; I see it makes a body valiant;
One neither feels Hunger nor Cold that is possest with it.

CLORIS - Thou art i'th' right, it can do Miracles.

GUILLIAM - So it seems, for without a Miracle you and I could never
Have rambled about these Woods all night without either Bottle or Wallet:
I could e'en cry for hunger now.

CLORIS - What a dull Soul this Fellow hath?
Sure it can never feel the generous Pains
Of Love, as mine does now; oh, how I glory
To find my Heart above the common rate!

Were not my Prince inconstant,
I would not envy what the Blessed do above:
But he is false, good Heaven! [Weeps. GUILLIAM - howls.
What dost thou feel, that thou shouldst weep with me?

GUILLIAM - Nothing but Hunger, sharp Hunger, forsooth.

CLORIS - Leave calling me forsooth, it will betray us.

GUILLIAM - What shall I call you then?

CLORIS - Call me, Philibert, or any thing;
And be familiar with me: put on thy Hat, lest any come and see us.

GUILLIAM - 'Tis a hard name, but I'll learn it by heart.
Well, Philibert - What shall we do when we come to Court?
[Puts on his Hat.
Besides eating and drinking, which I shall do in abundance.

CLORIS - We must get each of us a Service:
But thou art such a Clown.

GUILLIAM - Nay, say not so, honest Philibert: for look ye,
I am much the properer Fellow of the two.   [Walks.

CLORIS - Well, try thy fortune; but be sure you never discover
Me, whatever Questions may chance to be asked thee.

GUILLIAM - I warrant thee, honest Lad, I am true and trusty;
But I must be very familiar with you, you say.

CLORIS - Yes, before Company.

GUILLIAM - Pray let me begin and practise a little now,
An't please you, for fear I should not be saucy enough,
When we arrive at Court.

CLORIS - I'll warrant you you'll soon learn there.

GUILLIAM - Oh Lord, Philibert! Philibert! I see a Man a coming
Most deadly fine, let's run away.

CLORIS - Thus thou hast serv'd me all this night,
There's not a Bush we come at, but thou start'st thus.

GUILLIAM - 'Tis true you are a Lover, and may stay the danger on't;
But I'll make sure for one.

CLORIS - It is the Prince, oh Gods! what makes he here?
With Looks disorder'd too; this Place is fit for Death and sad
Despair; the melancholy Spring a sleepy murmur makes,

A proper Consort for departing Souls,
When mix'd with dying Groans, and the thick Boughs
Compose a dismal Roof;
Dark as the gloomy Shades of Death or Graves.
He comes this way, I'll hide my self awhile.   [Goes behind a Bush.

Enter Frederick.

FREDERICK - But yet not this, nor my despight to Laura,
Shall make me out of love with Life,
Whilst I have youthful Fires about my Heart:
Yet I must fight with Curtius,
And so chastise the Pride of that fond Maid,
Whose saucy Virtue durst controul my Flame.
And yet I love her not as I do Cloris;
But fain I would have overcome that Chastity,
Of which the foolish Beauty boasts so.

CLORIS - Curtius, I thank thee, now I do believe thee.
Guilliam, if thou seest any fighting anon,   [The Prince walks.
Be sure you run out and call some body.

GUILLIAM - You need not bid me run away, when I once
See them go to that.

Enter Curtius.

CURTIUS - Sir, I am come as you commanded me.

FREDERICK - When you consider what you've lately done,
You will not wonder why I sent for you;
And when I mean to fight, I do not use to parly:
Come draw.

CURTIUS - Shew me my Enemy, and then if I am slow

FREDERICK - I am he, needst thou one more powerful?

CURTIUS - You, Sir! what have I done to make you so?

FREDERICK - If yet thou want'st a further proof of it,
Know I'll dispute my Claim to Laura.

CURTIUS - That must not be with me, Sir;
God forbid that I should raise my Arm against my Prince.
If Laura have so little Faith and Virtue,
To render up that Right belongs to me,
With all my heart I yield her
To any but to you:
And, Sir, for your own sake you must not have her.

FREDERICK - Your Reason?

CURTIUS - Sir, you're already married.

FREDERICK - Thou lyest, and seek'st excuses for thy Cowardice.

CURTIUS - I wish you would recal that hasty Injury;
Yet this I'll bear from you, who know 'tis false.

FREDERICK - Will nothing move thee?

CURTIUS - You would believe so, Sir, if I should tell you,
That besides all this, I have a juster Cause.

FREDERICK - Juster than that of Laura? call it up, then,
And let it save thee from a further shame.

CURTIUS - Yes, so I will, 'tis that of Cloris,
Who needs my aids much more;
Do you remember such a Virgin, Sir?
For so she was till she knew Frederick,
The sweetest Innocent that ever Nature made.

FREDERICK - Not thy own Honour, nor thy Love to Laura,
Would make thee draw, and now at Cloris' Name
Thou art incens'd, thy Eyes all red with Rage:
Oh, thou hast rouz'd my Soul!
Nor would I justify my Wrongs to her,
Unless it were to satisfy my Jealousy,
Which thou hast rais'd in me by this concern.
Draw, or I'll kill thee.

CURTIUS - Stay, Sir, and hear me out.

FREDERICK - I will not stay, now I reflect on all
Thy former kindness to her -

CURTIUS - I will not fight, but I'll defend my self.   [They fight.

FREDERICK - We are betray'd.

CURTIUS - Yes, Sir, and you are wounded.
[GUILLIAM - runs bawling out, they are both wounded.

CLORIS - Oh Heaven defend the Prince!   [She peeps.

FREDERICK - I hear some coming, go, be gone,
And save thy self by flight.
[Frederick stands leaning on his Sword.

CURTIUS - Sir, give me leave to stay, my flight will look like Guilt.

FREDERICK - By no means, Curtius, thou wilt be taken here,
And thou shalt never charge me with that Crime of betraying
Thee: when we meet next, we'll end it.

CURTIUS - I must obey you then.   [Exit.

Enter Cloris.

CLORIS - Sir, has the Villain hurt you?   [She supports him.
Pray Heaven my Sorrows do not betray me now;
For since he's false, I fain would die conceal'd.   [Aside.
Shew me your Wound, and I will tie it up.
Alas, you bleed extremely.

FREDERICK - Kind Youth, thy Succours are in vain, though welcome;
For though I bleed, I am not wounded much.

CLORIS - No? why did you let him pass unpunish'd then,
Who would have hurt you more?

Enter Guilliam with Galliard.

GALLIARD - Where was't?

GUILLIAM - Look ye, Sir, there, don't you see them?

GALLIARD - How does your Highness? This Fellow told me
Of a quarrel here, which made me haste.

FREDERICK - Be silent, and carry me to my own apartment.

GALLIARD - Alas, Sir, is it you that fought?

FREDERICK - No more Questions.
Kind Boy, pray leave me not till I have found
A way to recompense thy pretty care of me.

CLORIS - I will wait on you, Sir.

[Exeunt all but Guilliam.

Enter Lorenzo and his Page. Peeps first.

LORENZO - What's the matter here? the Prince is wounded too.
Oh, what a Dog was I to know of some such thing,
And not secure them all?

[LORENZO - stands gazing at Guilliam. Guilliam stands tabering his Hat, and scruing his Face.

What's here? Ha, ha, ha, this is the pleasantest

Fellow that e'er I saw in my Life.
Prithee, Friend, what's thy Name?

GUILLIAM - My Name, an't shall like ye.
My Name, it is Guilliam.

LORENZO - From whence comest thou?

GUILLIAM - From a Village a great huge way off.

LORENZO - And what's thy business here, hah?

GUILLIAM - Truly, Sir, not to tell a Lye;
I come to get a Service here at Court.

LORENZO - A Service at Court! ha, ha, that's a pleasant
Humour, i'faith. Why, Fellow, what canst thou do?

GUILLIAM - Do, Sir! I can do any thing.

LORENZO - Why, what canst thou do? canst thou dress well?
Set a Peruke to advantage, tie a Crevat,
And Cuffs? put on a Belt with dexterity, hah?
These be the Parts that must recommend you.

GUILLIAM - I know not what you mean,
But I am sure I can do them all.

LORENZO - Thou art confident it seems, and I can tell
You, Sirrah, that's a great step to Preferment;
But well, go on then, canst ride the great Horse?

GUILLIAM - The biggest in all our Town
I have rid a thousand times.

LORENZO - That's well; canst fence?

GUILLIAM - Fence, Sir, what's that?

LORENZO - A Term we use for the Art and Skill of handling a Weapon.

GUILLIAM - I can thrash, Sir.

LORENZO - What's that, Man?

GUILLIAM - Why, Sir, it is, it is thrashing.

LORENZO - An Artist, I vow; canst play on any Musick?

GUILLIAM - Oh, most rogically, Sir, I have a Bagpipe that
Every Breath sets the whole Village a dancing.

LORENZO - Better still; and thou canst dance, I'll warrant?

GUILLIAM - Dance, he, he, he, I vow you've light on
My Master-piece, y'fegs.

LORENZO - And I'll try thee: Boy, go fetch some of the   [To the Page.
Musick hither which I keep in pay.   [Ex. Page.
But hark you, Friend, though I love Dancing very well,
And that may recommend thee in a great degree;
Yet 'tis wholly necessary that you should be valiant too:
We Great ones ought to be serv'd by Men of Valour,
For we are very liable to be affronted by many here
To our Faces, which we would gladly have beaten behind
Our Backs. But Pox on't, thou hast not the Huff
And Grimace of a Man of Prowess.

GUILLIAM - As for fighting, though I do not care for it,
Yet I can do't if any body angers me, or so.

LORENZO - But I must have you learn to do't when
Any body angers me too.

GUILLIAM - Sir, they told me I should have no need on't
Here; but I shall learn.

LORENZO - Why, you Fool, that's not a thing to be learn'd,
That's a brave Inclination born with Man,
A brave undaunted something, a thing that,
That comes from, from, I know not what,
For I was born without it.

Enter Page and Musick.

Oh, are you come? let's see, Sirrah, your Activity,
For I must tell you that's another step to Preferment.
[He dances a Jig en Paisant.
'Tis well perform'd; well, hadst thou but Wit,
Valour, Bone Mine, good Garb, a Peruke,
Conduct and Secrecy in Love-Affairs, and half
A dozen more good Qualities, thou wert
Fit for something; but I will try thee.
Boy, let him have better Clothes; as for his Documents,
I'll give him those my self.

GUILLIAM - Hah, I don't like that word, it sounds terribly.
[Aside.

[Exit Page and Guilliam with Musick.

LORENZO - This Fellow may be of use to me; being

Doubtless very honest, because he is so very simple:
For to say truth, we Men of Parts are sometimes
Over-wise, witness my last night's retreat
From but a supposed Danger, and returning to fall
Into a real one. Well, I'll now to Isabella,
And know her final Resolution; if Clarina will
Be kind, so; if not, there be those that will.
And though I cannot any Conquest boast
For all the Time and Money I have lost,
At least of Isabel I'll be reveng'd,
And have the flattering Baggage soundly swing'd;
And rather than she shall escape my Anger,
My self shall be the Hero that shall bang her.   [Exit.

ACT IV.

SCENE I. Antonio's House.

Enter Ismena and Isabella.

ISABELLA - Madam, turn your back to that side,
For there Antonio is hid; he must not see your
Face: now raise your Voice, that he may hear what 'tis you say.

ISMENA - I'll warrant you, Isabella:
Was ever wretched Woman's Fate like mine,
Forc'd to obey the rigid Laws of Parents,
And marry with a Man I did not love?

ANTONIO - Oh, there's my cause of Fear.   [Antonio peeps.

ISMENA - Though since I had him, thou know'st I have endeavour'd
To make his Will my Law,
Till by degrees and Custom, which makes things natural,
I found this Heart, which ne'er had been engag'd
To any other, grow more soft to him;
And still the more he lov'd, the more I was oblig'd,
And made returns still kinder; till I became
Not only to allow, but to repay his Tenderness.

ISABELLA - She counterfeits rarely.   [Aside.
Madam, indeed I have observ'd this truth.

ISMENA - See who 'tis knocks.   [One knocks.

ANTONIO - What will this come to?   [Aside.

ISABELLA - Madam, 'tis Alberto.

Enter Alberto. Bows.

ISMENA - My Lord, you've often told me that you lov'd me,
Which I with Womens usual Pride believ'd;
And now, encourag'd by my hopeful Promises,
You look for some Returns: Sir, is it so?

ALBERTO - What means she?
Pray Heaven I answer right.   [Aside.
Madam, if I have err'd in that belief,
To know I do so, is sufficient punishment.
Lovers, Madam, though they have no returns,
Like sinking Men, still catch at all they meet with;
And whilst they live, though in the midst of Storms,
Because they wish, they also hope for Calms.

ISMENA - And did you, Sir, consider who I was?

ALBERTO - Yes, Madam, Wife unto my Friend Antonio,
The only Man that has an Interest here:
But, Madam, that must still submit to Love.

ISMENA - Canst thou at once be true to him and me?

ALBERTO - Madam, I know not that;
But since I must lose one,
My Friendship I can better lay aside.

ISMENA - Hast thou forgot how dear thou art to him?

ALBERTO - No, I do believe I am, and that his Life
Were but a worthless trifle, if I needed it.
Yet, Madam, you are dearer to him still
Than his Alberto; and 'tis so with me:
Him I esteem, but you I do adore;
And he whose Soul's insensible of Love,
Can never grateful to his Friendship prove.

ISMENA - By your example, Sir, I'll still retain
My Love for him; and what I had for you,
Which was but Friendship, I'll abandon too.

ANTONIO - Happy Antonio.   [Aside.

ISMENA - Pray what have you Antonio cannot own?
Has he not equal Beauty, if not exceeding thine?
Has he not equal Vigour, Wit, and Valour?
And all that even raises Men to Gods,
Wert not for poor Mortality?
Vain Man, couldst thou believe
That I would quit my Duty to this Husband,

And sacrifice his Right to thee?
Couldst thou believe me yesterday?
When from thy Importunity and Impudence,
To send thee from me,
I promised thee to love thee.
Nay, rather, treacherous Man,
Couldst thou believe I did not hate thee then,
Who basely would betray thy Friend and me?

ALBERTO - Sure this is earnest.   [Aside.

ANTONIO - Oh brave Clarina!   [Aside.

ISMENA - Speak, Traitor to my Fame and Honour;
Was there no Woman, but Antonio's Wife,
With whom thou couldst commit so foul a Crime?
And none but he to bring to publick Shame?
A Man who trusted thee, and lov'd thee too?
Speak and if yet thou hast a sense of Virtue,
Call to the Saints for pardon, or thou dy'st.
[She draws a Poniard, and runs at him; he steps back to avoid it.

ALBERTO - Hold, Clarina! I am amaz'd.

ISMENA - But stay.
Thou say'st my Beauty forc'd thee to this Wickedness,
And that's the cause you have abus'd Antonio.
Nor is it all the Power I have with him,
Can make him credit what I tell him of thee;
And should I live, I still must be pursu'd by thee,
And unbeliev'd by him:
Alberto, thou shalt ne'er be guilty more,
Whilst this and this may meet.
[Offering to wound her self, is stay'd by Alberto and Isabella. They set Ismena in a Chair; Alberto kneels weeping.

ALBERTO - Hold, my divine Clarina.

ANTONIO - Shall I discover my self, or steal away?   [Aside.
And all asham'd of Life after this Action,
Go where the Sun or Day may never find me?
Oh! what Virtue I've abus'd
Curse on my little Faith;
And all the Curses Madness can invent,
Light on my groundless Jealousy.   [Ex. Antonio.

ALBERTO - Clarina, why so cruel to my Heart?
'Tis true, I love you, but with as chaste an Ardour,
As Souls departing pay the Deities,
When with incessant Sighs they haste away,
And leave Humanity behind. Oh! so did I

Abandon all the lesser Joys of Life,
For that of being permitted but t'adore ye.
Alas, if 'twere displeasing to you,
Why did your self encourage it?
I might have languish'd, as I did before,
And hid those Crimes which make you hate me now.
Oh, I am lost? Antonio, thou'st undone me;   [He rises in Rage.
Hear me, Ungrate; I swear by all that's good,
I'll wash away my Mischief with thy Blood.

ISABELLA - Antonio hears you not, Sir, for he's departed.

ISMENA - Is Antonio gone?
[She looks pertly up, who before lay half dead.

ALBERTO - How's this, has she but feign'd?

ISMENA - Know it was but feign'd; I hope this proof
Of what I've promis'd you, does not displease you.

ALBERTO - Am I thus fortunate, thus strangely happy?

ISMENA - Time will confirm it to you, go, do not
Now thank me for't, but seek Antonio out;
Perhaps he may have too great a Sense of the
Mischiefs his Jealousies had like to have caus'd:
But conjure him to take no notice of what's past to me;
This easy slight of mine secures our Fears,
And serves to make Antonio confident,
Who now will unbelieve his Eyes and Ears;
And since before, when I was innocent,
He could suspect my Love and Duty too,
I'll try what my dissembling it will do.
Go haste.

ALBERTO - Madam, I go, surpriz'd with Love and Wonder.   [Ex. Alberto.

ISMENA - You'll be more surpriz'd, when you know   [Aside.
That you are cheated too as well as Antonio.

[Exeunt.

SCENE II. A Street.

Enter Curtius disguis'd in a black Peruke and Beard, with Pietro disguised also.

CURTIUS - Well, what hast thou learn'd?

PIETRO - News enough, Sir, but none good;
That the Prince's Wounds are small,

So that he intends to take the Air this Evening;
That he sollicits Laura hard;
And, Sir, that you are proclaim'd Traitor.

CURTIUS - So, what says the Messenger you sent to Cloris?

PIETRO - Sir, he brings sad tidings back.

CURTIUS - What tidings? is she dead?
That would revive my Soul,
And fortify my easy Nature with some wicked Notions,
As deep as those this flattering Prince made use of,
When he betray'd my Sister, pretty Cloris:
Come, speak it boldly, for nothing else
Will make me do her Justice.

PIETRO - No, Sir, she is not dead,
But fled, and none knows whither;
Only Guilliam attends her.

CURTIUS - Worse and worse; but what of Laura?

PIETRO - She, Sir, is kept a Prisoner by her Father,
And speaks with none but those that come from Frederick.

CURTIUS - Laura confin'd too! 'tis time to hasten then,
With my, till now, almost disarmed Revenge:
Thus I may pass unknown the Streets of Florence,
And find an opportunity to reach this Prince's Heart,
Oh, Vengeance! luxurious Vengeance!
Thy Pleasures turn a Rival to my Love,
And make the mightier Conquest o'er my Heart.
Cloris, I will revenge thy Tears and Sufferings;
And to secure the Doom of him that wrong'd thee,
I'll call on injur'd Laura too.
Here take these Pictures and where thou see'st   [Gives him Boxes.
A knot of Gallants, open one or two, as if by stealth,
To gaze upon the Beauties, and then straight close them
But stay, here comes the only Man
I could have wish'd for; he'll proclaim my Business
Better than a Picture or a Trumpet.   [They stand by.
[Curtius takes back the Pictures.

Enter Lorenzo and Guilliam dressed in fineish Clothes, but the same high-crown'd Hat.

LORENZO - Did, ha, ha, ha, did, ha, ha; did ever any
Mortal Man behold such a Figure as thou art now?
Well, I see 'tis a damnable thing not to
Be born a Gentleman; the Devil himself
Can never make thee truly jantee now.
Come, come, come forward; these Clothes become

Thee, as a Saddle does a Sow; why com'st thou not?
Why - ha, ha, I hope thou hast not
Hansel'd thy new Breeches,
Thou look'st so filthily on't.   [He advances, looking sourly.

GUILLIAM - No, Sir, I hope I have more manners than so;
But if I should, 'tis not my fault;
For the necessary Houses are hard
To be met withal here at Court.

LORENZO - Very well, Sirrah; you begin already to be
Witty with the Court: but I can tell you, it has as
Many necessary Places in't, as any Court in Christendom
But what a Hat thou hast?

GUILLIAM - Why, Sir, though I say't, this is accounted of
In our Village; but I had another but now,
Which I blew off in a high Wind; and I never mist it,
Till I had an occasion to pluck it off to a young
Squire, they call a Lacquey; and, Fegs,
I had none at all: and because I would not lose
My Leg for want of a Hat, I fetch'd this;
And I can tell you, Sir, it has a fashionable Brim.

LORENZO - A Fool's head of your own, has it not?
The Boys will hoot at us as we pass, hah,
Who be these, who be these   [Goes towards Curtius and Pietro.

Curtius – Here, this to Don Alonso, this to the
English Count; and this you may shew to the
Young German Prince and this
I will reserve for higher Prices.   [Gives Pietro Pictures.

PIETRO - Will you shew none to the Courtiers, Sir?

CURTIUS - Away, you Fool, I deal in no such Trash.

LORENZO - How, Sir, how was that? pray how came we to
Gain your dis-favour?

CURTIUS - I cry you mercy, Sir, pray what are you;

LORENZO - A Courtier, Sir, I can assure you,
And one of the best Rank too;
I have the Prince's ear, Sir.
What have you there, hah? Pictures? let me see
What, are they to be bought?

CURTIUS - Sir, they are Copies of most fair Originals,
Not to be bought but hired.

LORENZO - Say you so, Friend? the Price, the Price.

CURTIUS - Five thousand Crowns a Month, Sir.

LORENZO - The Price is somewhat saucy.

CURTIUS - Sir, they be curious Pieces, were never blown upon,
Have never been in Courts, nor hardly Cities.

LORENZO - Upon my word, that's considerable;
Friend, pray where do they live?

CURTIUS - In the Piazzo, near the Palace.

LORENZO - Well, put up your Ware, shew not a face of them
Till I return! for I will bring you
The best Chapman in all Florence,
Except the Duke himself.

CURTIUS - You must be speedy then,
For I to morrow shall be going towards Rome.

LORENZO - A subtle Rascal this: thou think'st, I warrant,
To make a better Market amongst the Cardinals.
But take my word, ne'er a Cardinal of them all
Comes near this Man, I mean, to bring you in
Matters of Beauty, so, this will infallibly make
My Peace again: [Aside.] Look ye, Friend
Be ready, for 'tis the Prince, the noble generous Frederick,
That I design your Merchant.   [Goes out.

CURTIUS - Your Servant, Sir, that is Guilliam;
I cannot be mistaken in him, go call him back.
[Pietro fetches him back, who puts on a surly Face.
Friend, what art thou?

GUILLIAM - What am I? why, what am I? dost thou not see
What I am? a Courtier, Friend.

CURTIUS - But what's thy Name?

GUILLIAM - My Name, I have not yet considered.

CURTIUS - What was thy Name?

GUILLIAM - What was my Name?

CURTIUS - Yes, Friend, thou hadst one.

GUILLIAM - Yes, Friend, thou hadst one.

CURTIUS - Dog, do'st eccho me? do'st thou repeat?
I say again, what is thy Name?   [Shakes him.

GUILLIAM - Oh horrible! why, Sir, it was Guilliam
When I was a silly Swain.

Curtius – Guilliam, the same;
Didst thou not know a Maid whose name was Cloris?

GUILLIAM - Yes, there was such a Maid,
But now she's none!

CURTIUS - Was such a Maid, but now she's none!
The Slave upbraids my Griefs.   [Aside.

GUILLIAM - Yes, Sir, so I said.

CURTIUS - So you said!

GUILLIAM - Why, yes, Sir, what, do you repeat?

CURTIUS - What mean you, Sirrah? have you a mind to
Have your Throat cut? tell me where she is.

GUILLIAM - I dare as well be hang'd.
Now must I devise a lye, or never look Cloris
In the Face more.   [Aside.

CURTIUS - Here's Gold for thee; I will be secret too.

GUILLIAM - Oh, Sir, the poor Maid you speak of is dead.

CURTIUS - Dead! where dy'd she? and how?

GUILLIAM - Now am I put to my wits; this 'tis to begin
In Sin, as our Curate said: I must go on: [Aside.
Why, Sir, she came into the Wood and hard by a
River-side, she sigh'd, and she wept full sore;
And cry'd two or three times out upon Curtius,
And then -   [Howls.

CURTIUS - Poor Cloris, thy Fate was too severe.

GUILLIAM - And then as I was saying, Sir,
She leapt into the River, and swam up the Stream.   [Curtius weeps.

PIETRO - And why up the Stream, Friend?

GUILLIAM - Because she was a Woman and that's all.   [Ex. Guilliam.

CURTIUS - Farewel, and thank thee.

Poor Cloris dead, and banish'd too from Laura!
Was ever wretched Lover's Fate like mine!
And he who injures me, has power to do so;
But why, where lies this Power about this Man?
Is it his Charms of Beauty, or of Wit?
Or that great Name he has acquir'd in War?
Is it the Majesty, that holy something,
That guards the Person of this Demi-god?
This awes not me, there must be something more.
For ever, when I call upon my Wrongs,
Something within me pleads so kindly for him,
As would persuade me that he could not err.
Ah, what is this? where lies this Power divine,
That can so easily make a Slave of mine?

[Exeunt.

SCENE III. Frederick's Chamber.

Enter Frederick, and Cloris finely dress'd.

FREDERICK - 'Tis much methinks, a Boy of so dejected,
Humble Birth, should have so much of Sense
And Soul about him.

CLORIS - I know not that; but if I have a thought
Above that humble Birth or Education,
It was inspir'd by Love.

FREDERICK - Still you raise my Wonder greater;
Thou a Lover?

CLORIS - Yes, my Lord, though I am young,
I've felt the power of Beauty;
And should you look upon the Object, Sir,
Your Wonders soon would cease;
Each Look does even animate Insensibles,
And strikes a reverend Awe upon the Soul:
Nothing is found so lovely.

FREDERICK - Thou speak'st prettily, I think Love
Indeed has inspir'd thee.

CLORIS - These were the Flatteries, Sir, she us'd to me;
Of her it was I learn'd to speak, and sigh,
And look, as oft you say, I do on you.

FREDERICK - Why then, it seems she made returns?

CLORIS - Ah! Sir, 'twas I that first was blest,

I first the happy Object was belov'd;
For, 'twas a Person, Sir, so much above me,
It had been Sin to've rais'd my Eyes to her;
Or by a glance, or sigh, betray my Pain.
But Oh! when with a thousand soft Expressions,
She did encourage me to speak of Love!
My God! how soon extravagant I grew,
And told so oft the story of my Passion,
That she grew weary of the repeated Tale,
And punish'd my presumption with a strange neglect.   [Weeps.

FREDERICK - How, my good Philibert?

CLORIS - Would suffer me to see her Face no more.

FREDERICK - That was pity; without a Fault?

CLORIS - Alas, Sir, I was guilty of no Crime,
But that of having told her how I lov'd her;
For all I had I sacrific'd to her;
Poor worthless Treasures to any but a Lover;
And such you know accept the meanest things,
Which Love and a true Devotion do present.
When she was present, I found a thousand ways
To let her know how much I was her Slave;
And absent, still invented new ones,
And quite neglected all my little Business;
Counting the tedious Moments of the Day
By Sighs and Tears; thought it an Age to night,
Whose Darkness might secure our happy meeting:
But we shall meet no more on these kind Terms.   [Sighs.

FREDERICK - Come, do not weep, sweet Youth, thou art too young,
To have thy blooming Cheeks blasted with sorrow;
Thou wilt out-grow this childish Inclination,
And shalt see Beauties here, whose every glance
Kindle new Fires, and quite expel the old.

CLORIS - Oh, never, Sir.

FREDERICK - When I was first in love, I thought so too,
But now with equal ardour
I doat upon each new and beauteous Object.

CLORIS - And quite forget the old?

FREDERICK - Not so; but when I see them o'er again,
I find I love them as I did before.

CLORIS - Oh God forbid, I should be so inconstant!
No, Sir, though she be false, she has my Heart,

And I can die, but not redeem the Victim.

FREDERICK - Away, you little Fool, you make me sad
By this resolve: but I'll instruct you better.

CLORIS - I would not make you sad for all the World.
Sir, I will sing, or dance, do any thing
That may divert you.

FREDERICK - I thank thee, Philibert, and will accept
Thy Bounty; perhaps it may allay thy Griefs awhile too.

CLORIS - I'll call the Musick, Sir.   [She goes out.

FREDERICK - This Boy has strange agreements in him.

Enter Cloris with Musick.

She bids them play, and dances a Jig.

This was wondrous kind, my pretty Philibert.

[Exeunt Musick.

Enter Page.

PAGE - Lorenzo, my Lord, begs admittance.

FREDERICK - He may come in.   [Exit Page.

Enter Lorenzo.

Well, Lorenzo, what's the News with thee?
How goes the price of Beauty, hah?

LORENZO - My Lord, that question is a propos to
What I have to say; this Paper will answer your
Question, Sir -   [Gives him a Paper, he reads.
Hah, I vow to gad a lovely Youth;   [Lorenzo gazes on Phil.
But what makes he here with Frederick?
This Stripling may chance to mar my market of Women now
'Tis a fine Lad, how plump and white he is;   [Aside.
Would I could meet him somewhere i'th' dark,
I'd have a fling at him, and try whether I
Were right Florentine.

FREDERICK - Well, Sir, where be these Beauties?

LORENZO - I'll conduct you to them.

FREDERICK - What's the Fellow that brings them?

LORENZO - A Grecian, I think, or something.

FREDERICK - Beauties from Greece, Man!

LORENZO - Why, let them be from the Devil,
So they be new and fine, what need we care?
But you must go to night.

FREDERICK - I am not in a very good condition
To make Visits of that kind.

LORENZO - However, see them, and if you like them,
You may oblige the Fellow to a longer stay,
For I know they are handsome.

FREDERICK - That's the only thing thou art judge of;
Well, go you and prepare them;
And Philibert, thou shalt along with me;
I'll have thy Judgment too.

CLORIS - Good Heaven, how false he is!   [Aside.

LORENZO - What time will your Highness come?

FREDERICK - Two Hours hence.   [Ex. Frederick.

LORENZO - So then I shall have time to have a bout
With this jilting Huswife Isabella,
For my Fingers itch to be at her.   [Aside.   [Ex. Lorenzo.

CLORIS - Not know me yet? cannot this Face inform him?
My Sighs, nor Eyes, my Accent, nor my Tale?
Had he one thought of me, he must have found me out.
Yes, yes, 'tis certain I am miserable;
He's going now to see some fresher Beauties,
And I, he says, must be a witness of it;
This gives me Wounds, painful as those of Love:
Some Women now would find a thousand Plots
From so much Grief as I have, but I'm dull;
Yet I'll to Laura, and advise with her,
Where I will tell her such a heavy Tale,
As shall oblige her to a kind concern:
This may do; I'll tell her of this Thought,
This is the first of Art I ever thought on;
And if this proves a fruitless Remedy,
The next, I need not study, how to die.

[Exeunt.

SCENE IV. A Street.

Enter Lorenzo, meets Guilliam, who passes by him, and takes no notice of him.

LORENZO - How now, Manners a few?

GUILLIAM - I cry you heartily, Sir, I did not see you.

LORENZO - Well, Sirrah, the News.

GUILLIAM - Sir, the Gentlewoman whom you sent me to says
That she'll meet you here.

LORENZO - That's well, thou mayst come to be a States-man
In time, thou art a fellow of so quick dispatch: But hark ye,
Sirrah, there are a few
Lessons I must learn you,
Concerning Offices of this nature;
But another time for that: but -
[Whispers.

Enter Isabella, and Antonio's Valet.

ISABELLA - Here he is; and prithee, when thou seest him in
My Chamber, go and tell my Lord,
Under pretence of the care you have of the
Honour of his House.

VALET - I warrant you, let me alone for a Tale,
And a Lye at the end on't; which shall not over-much
Incense him, nor yet make him neglect coming.
[Exit Valet

LORENZO - Oh, are you there, Mistress? what have you now
To say for your last Night's Roguery?
Are not you a Baggage? confess.

ISABELLA - You have a mind to lose your opportunity again,
As you did last Night, have ye not? Pray God your own
Shadow scare you not, As it did then; and you will possibly believe
No body meant you harm then, nor now.

LORENZO - Art thou in earnest?

ISABELLA - Are you in earnest?

LORENZO - Yes, that I am, and that Clarina shall find,
If I once come to her.

ISABELLA - Come, leave your frippery Jests, and come in.

LORENZO - Guilliam, be sure you attend me here,
And whoever you see, saynothing; the best on't is,
Thou art not much known.
[ISABELLA - and LORENZO - go in.

GUILLIAM - Well, I see there is nothing but foutering
In this Town; wou'd our Lucia were here too for me,
For all the Maids I meet with are so giglish
And scornful, that a Man, as I am,
Gets nothing but flouts and flings from them.
Oh, for the little kind Lass that lives
Under the Hill, of whom the Song was made;
Which because I have nothing else to do,
I will sing over now; hum, hum.

The Song for Guilliam.   [To some Tune like him.

In a Cottage by the Mountain
Lives a very pretty Maid,
Who lay sleeping by a Fountain,
Underneath a Myrtle shade;
Her Petticoat of wanton Sarcenet,
The amorous Wind about did move,
And quite unveil'd,
And quite unveil'd the Throne of Love,
And quite unveil'd the Throne of Love.

'Tis something cold, I'll go take a Niperkin of Wine,

[Goes out.

Enter Isabella and Lorenzo above, as frighted into the Balcony.

LORENZO - This was some trick of thine, I will be hang'd else.

ISABELLA - Oh, I'll be sworn you wrong me;
Alas, I'm undone by't.   [Antonio at the Door knocks.

ANTONIO - Open the Door, thou naughty Woman.

LORENZO - Oh, oh, what shall I do? what shall I do?

ANTONIO - Open the Door, I say.

LORENZO - Oh, 'tis a damnable leap out at this Balcony.

ISABELLA - And yet you are a dead Man, if you see him.

ANTONIO - Impudence, will you open the Door?

ISABELLA - I will, Sir, immediately.

LORENZO - Devise some way to let me down,
Or I will throw thee out; no Ladder of Ropes, no Device?
If a Man would not forswear Whoring for the future
That is in my condition, I am no true Gentleman.

ANTONIO - Open, or I will break the Door.

ISABELLA - Hold the Door, and swear lustily that you
Are my Husband, and I will in the mean time
Provide for your safety,
Though I can think of none but the Sheets from the Bed.

[He holds the Door.

LORENZO - Any thing to save my Life;
Sir, you may believe me upon my Honour,
I am lawful Husband to Isabella,
And have no designs upon your House or Honour.

[ISABELLA - this while fastens the Sheets, which are to be suppos'd from the Bed, to the Balcony.

ANTONIO - Thou art some Villain.

LORENZO - No, Sir, I am an honest Man, and married lawfully.

ANTONIO - Who art thou?

LORENZO - Hast thou done?

ISABELLA - Yes, but you must venture hard.

ISABELLA - 'Tis Lorenzo, Sir.

LORENZO - A Pox on her, now am I asham'd to all eternity.

ISABELLA - Sir, let me beg you'l take his
Word and Oath to night,
And to morrow I will satisfy you.

[LORENZO - gets down by the Sheets.

ANTONIO - Look you make this good,
Or you shall both dearly pay for't.

LORENZO - I am alive, yes, yes, all's whole and sound,
Which is a mercy, I can tell you;
This is whoring now: may I turn Franciscan,
If I could not find in my heart to do penance
In Camphire Posset, this Month, for this.
Well, I must to this Merchant of Love,

And I would gladly be there before the Prince:
For since I have mist here,
I shall be amorous enough,
And then I'll provide for Frederick;
For 'tis but just, although he be my Master,
That I in these Ragousts should be his Taster.

[Exeunt.

SCENE V. Antonio's House.

Enter Ismena with a Veil.

ISMENA - Alberto is not come yet, sure he loves me;
But 'tis not Tears, and Knees, that can confirm me;
No, I must be convinc'd by better Argument.
Deceit, if ever thou a Guide wert made
To amorous Hearts, assist a Love-sick Maid.

Enter Alberto.

ALBERTO - Your pleasure, Madam?
Oh that she would be brief,
And send me quickly from her,
For her Eyes will overthrow my purpose.   [Aside.

ISMENA - Alberto, do you love me?

ALBERTO - No.

ISMENA - No! have you deceiv'd me then?

ALBERTO - Neither, Clarina; when I told you so,
By Heaven, 'twas perfect Truth.

ISMENA - And what have I done since should
Merit your Dis-esteem?

ALBERTO - Nothing but what has rais'd it.

ISMENA - To raise your Esteem, then it seems, is
To lessen your Love; or, as most Gallants are,
You're but pleas'd with what you have not;
And love a Mistress with great Passion, till you find
Your self belov'd again, and then you hate her.

ALBERTO - You wrong my Soul extremely,
'Tis not of that ungrateful nature;
To love me is to me a greater Charm
Than that of Wit or Beauty.

ISMENA - I'm glad on't, Sir; then
I have pleasant News for you,
I know a Lady, and a Virgin too,
That loves you with such Passion,
As has oblig'd me to become her Advocate.

ALBERTO - I am very much oblig'd to her,
If there be any such.

ISMENA - Upon my Life, there is; I am in earnest,
The Lady is my Sister too.

ALBERTO - How, Clarina, this from you?

ISMENA - Nay, I have promis'd her, that you shall love her too,
Since both her Birth and Beauty merits you.

ALBERTO - Away, false Woman: I love your Sister!
No, I will hate ye both.

ISMENA - Why so Angry?
Alas, it is against my Will I do it.

ALBERTO - Did you betray my Faith, when 'twas so easy
To give a credit to your tale of Love?
Oh Woman, faithless Woman!

ISMENA - Alberto, with a world of shame I own
That I then lov'd you, and must do so still:
But since that Love must be accounted criminal,
And that a world of danger does attend it;
I am resolv'd, though I can never quit it,
To change it into kind Esteem for you;
And would ally you, Sir, as near to me,
As our unkind Stars will permit me.

ALBERTO - I thank you, Madam: Oh, what a shame it is,
To be out-done in Virtue, as in Love!

ISMENA - Another favour I must beg of you,
That you will tell Antonio what is past.

ALBERTO - How mean you, Madam?

ISMENA - Why, that I love you, Sir,
And how I have deceiv'd him into confidence.

ALBERTO - This is strange; you cannot mean it sure.

ISMENA - When I intend to be extremely good,

I would not have a secret Sin within,
Though old, and yet repented too: no, Sir,
Confession always goes with Penitence.

ALBERTO - Do you repent you that you lov'd me then?

ISMENA - Not so; but that I did abuse Antonio.

ALBERTO - And can you think that this will cure his Jealousy?

ISMENA - Doubtless it will, when he knows how needless 'tis;
For when they're most secure, they're most betray'd:
Besides, I did but act the part he made;
And Ills he forces, sure he'll not upbraid.
Go seek out Antonio.

ALBERTO - You have o'ercome me, Madam, every way,
And this your last Command I can obey;
Your Sister too I'll see, and will esteem,
But you've my Heart, which I can ne'er redeem.

[Exeunt severally.

ACT V.

SCENE I. Laura's Chamber.

Enter Laura and Cloris like a Boy, as before.

LAURA - Forward, dear Cloris.

CLORIS - And, Madam, 'twas upon a Holyday,
It chanc'd Prince Frederick came into our Village,
On some reports were made him of my Beauty,
Attended only by the noble Curtius:
They found me in the Church at my Devotion,
Whom Frederick soon distinguished from the rest;
He kneel'd down by me, and instead of Prayer,
He fell to praise but 'twas my Beauty only;
That I could tell you, of my strange surprize!
My Zeal was all disordered, and my Eyes
Fed on the false, not real Sacrifice.
I wanted Art my Sentiments to hide,
Which from my Eyes and Blushes soon he spy'd.

LAURA - And did you know him then?

CLORIS - Not till he left me:
But, to be short, Madam, we parted there;

But e'er he went he whisper'd in my ear,
And sigh'd, Ah, Cloris! e'er you do depart,
Tell me, where 'tis you will dispose my Heart?
Pray give me leave to visit it again,
Your Eyes that gave can only ease my Pain.
I, only blushing, gave him my consent;
He paid his Thanks in Sighs, and from me went.
That night, alas, I took but little rest;
The new and strange Disorder in my Breast
Can, Madam, only by your self be guest.

LAURA - I'll not deny that I'm a Lover too,
And can imagine what was felt by you.

CLORIS - No sooner did the welcome Day appear,
But Lucia brought me word the Prince was there;
His very Name disorder'd me much more,
Than did his Sight or Touch the day before;
So soon my rising Love grew up to power,
So soon he did become my Conqueror.
How pale and trembling, when he did appear,
I grew, he too had marks of Love and Fear.
But I'll omit the many visits paid,
Th' unvalued Presents, and the Oaths he made,
My kind Disputes on all his Letters writ,
How all my Doubts were answer'd by his Wit;
How oft he vow'd to marry me, whilst I
Durst not believe the pleasing Perjury:
And only tell you, that one night he came,
Led by designs of an impatient Flame;
When all the House was silently asleep,
Except my self, who Love's sad Watch did keep;
Arm'd with his Ponyard, and his Breast all bare,
His Face all pale with restless Love and Fear;
So many wild and frantick things he said,
And so much Grief and Passion too betray'd,
So often vow'd he'd finish there his Life,
If I refus'd him to become his Wife;
That I half-dying, said it should be so;
Which though I fear'd, Oh, how I wish'd it too!
Both prostrate on the Ground i'th' face of Heaven,
His Vows to me, and mine to him were given:
And then, oh, then, what did I not resign!
With the assurance that the Prince was mine.   [Weeps.

LAURA - Poor Cloris, how I pity thee!
Since Fate has treated me with equal rigor;
Curtius is banish'd, Frederick still pursues me,
And by a cruel Father I'm confin'd,
And cannot go to serve my self or thee.   [One knocks.

LORENZO - [Without.] Sister Laura, Sister.

LAURA - It is my Brother, would he would be kind,
And set us free; he shall not see thee,
And I'll persuade him.

[As she puts Cloris into her Closet, enter Lorenzo with a Letter.

LORENZO - Hah, locking her Closet! now, were I a right
Italian, should I grow jealous, and enrag'd at
I know not what: hah, Sister!
What are you doing here?
Open your Cabinet, and let me see't.

LAURA - Sir, 'tis in disorder, and not worth your seeing now.

LORENZO - 'Tis so, I care not for that, I'll see't.

LAURA - Pray do not, Brother.

LORENZO - Your denial makes me the more inquisitive.

LAURA - 'Tis but my saying, he came from the Prince,
And he dares not take it ill.   [Aside.
Here, Sir,   [Gives him the Key.

LORENZO - And here's for you too; a Letter from Curtius,
And therefore I would not open it: I took it up
At the Post-house.   [She reads, and seems pleas'd.
Now if this should prove some surly Gallant of hers,
And give me a slash o'er the Face for peeping
I were but rightly serv'd;
And why the Devil should I expect my Sister should
Have more Virtue than my self?
She's the same flesh and blood: or why, because
She's the weaker Vessel,
Should all the unreasonable burden of the Honour
Of our House, as they call it,
Be laid on her Shoulders, whilst we may commit
A thousand Villanies? but 'tis so
Here, open the Door;
I'll put her before me, however.
[She opens the Door, and brings out Cloris.

LAURA - Sir, 'tis Philibert from the Prince.

LORENZO - Why, how now, Youngster, I see you intend
To thrive by your many Trades;
So soon, so soon, i'faith? but, Sirrah,
This is my Sister, and your Prince's Mistress;
Take notice of that.

CLORIS - I know not what you mean.

LORENZO - Sir, you cannot deceive me so;
And you were right serv'd, you would be made fit
For nothing but the great Turk's Seraglio.

CLORIS - You mistake my business, Sir.

LORENZO - Your Blushes give you the lye, Sirrah;
But for the Prince's sake, and another reason I have,
I will pardon you for once.

LAURA - He has not done a fault, and needs it not.

LORENZO - Was he not alone with thee?
And is not that enough? Well, I see I am no Italian
In Punctillio's of honourable Revenge.
There is but one experiment left to prove my self so;
And if that fail, I'll e'en renounce my Country.
Boy, harkye, there is a certain kindness
You may do me, and get your pardon for being found here.

CLORIS - You shall command me any thing.

LORENZO - Prithee how long hast thou been set up for thy self, Hah?

CLORIS - As how, Sir?

LORENZO - Poh, thou understand'st me.

CLORIS - Indeed I do not, Sir; what is't you mean?

LORENZO - A smooth-fac'd Boy, and ask such a Question?
Fy, fy, this Ignorance was ill counterfeited
To me that understand the World.

CLORIS - Explain yourself, Sir.

LORENZO - Lookye, ten or twenty Pistoles will do you
No hurt, will it?

CLORIS - Not any, Sir.

LORENZO - Why, so, 'tis well anything will make thee
Apprehend.

CLORIS - I shall be glad to serve you, Sir, without that fee.

LORENZO - That's kindly said
I see a Man must not be too easy of belief: had I been so,

This Boy would have been at, what d'ye mean, Sir?
And, Lord, I understand you not.
Well, Philibert, here's earnest to bind the Bargain;
I am now in haste; when I see thee next,
I'll tell thee more.   [Lorenzo whispers to Laura.

CLORIS - This 'tis to be a Favourite now;
I warrant you I must do him some good office to the Prince,
Which I'll be sure to do.

LORENZO - Nay, it must be done, for she has us'd me basely;
Oh, 'tis a Baggage.

LAURA - Let me alone to revenge you on Isabella,
Get me but from this Imprisonment.

LORENZO - I will: whilst I hold the old Man in a dispute,
Do you two get away; but be sure thou pay'st her home.

LAURA - I warrant you, Sir, this was happy;
Now shall I see Curtius.

LORENZO - Philibert, I advise you to have a care of
Wenching: 'twill spoil a good Face,
And mar your better market of the two.   [Ex. Lorenzo.

LAURA - Come, let us haste, and by the way, I'll tell thee
Of a means that may make us all happy.

[Exeunt.

SCENE II. A Grove.

Enter Alberto melancholy.

ALBERTO - Antonio said he would be here,
I'm impatient till he come -

Enter Antonio.

ANTONIO - Alberto, I have such a Project for thee!

ALBERTO - Hah -   [Gazes.

ANTONIO - What ails thee, art thou well?

ALBERTO - No.

ANTONIO - Where art thou sick?

ALBERTO - At Heart, Antonio, poison'd by thy Jealousy;
Oh, thou hast ruin'd me, undone my Quiet,
And from a Man of reasonable Virtue,
Hast brought me to a wild distracted Lover.

ANTONIO - Explain your self.

ALBERTO - Thou'st taught me, Friend, to love Clarina;
Not, as I promis'd thee, to feign, but so,
That I, unless I do possess that Object,
I think must die; at best be miserable.

ANTONIO - How, Sir, have I done this?

ALBERTO - Yes, Antonio, thou hast done this.

ANTONIO - My dear Alberto, said you that you lov'd her?

ALBERTO - Yes, Antonio, against my will I do;
As much against my will, as when I told her so;
Urg'd by thy needless Stratagem.

ANTONIO - Name it no more, it was an idle Fault,
Which I do so repent me,
That if you find I should relapse again,
Kill me, and let me perish with my Weakness:
And were that true you tell me of your Passion,
Sure I should wish to die, to make you happy.

ALBERTO - That's kindly said, and I submit to you,
And am content to be out-done in Amity.

ANTONIO - Yes, I'll resign my Claims, and leave the World;
Alberto, 'tis unkind to think I would be happy
By ways must ruin you:
But sure you tell me this, but only to afflict me.

ALBERTO - 'Tis truth, Antonio, I do love Clarina;
And, what is yet far worse for thy repose,
Believe my self so bless'd to be belov'd.

ANTONIO - How, to be belov'd by her!
Oh dire effects of Jealousy!

ALBERTO - All that you saw to day was only feign'd,
To let you see, that even your Eyes and Ears
Might be impos'd upon.

ANTONIO - Can it be possible!

ALBERTO - And now she thinks she is enough reveng'd;

And lets you know, in her feign'd Scorn to me,
That all your Sleights and Cunnings are but vain:
She has deceiv'd them all, and by that Art,
Gives you a Confidence, and me a Heart.

ANTONIO - I must confess, it is but just in her
To punish thus the Errors of my Fear;
I do forgive her, from my Soul I do.
But, Sir, what satisfaction's this to you?

ALBERTO - Clarina happy, I'll from Court retire,
And by that Absence quench my Hopeless Fire:
War I will make my Mistress, who may be,
Perhaps, more kind than she has been to me;
Where though I cannot conquer, 'twill allow
That I may die; that's more than this will do.

ANTONIO - Why did you, Sir, betray my Weakness to her?
Though 'twas but what I did deserve from you.

ALBERTO - By all that's good, she knew the Plot before,
From Isabella, who it seems o'erheard us,
When you once press'd me to't:
And had we wanted Virtue, thoud'st been lost.

ANTONIO - I own the Crime;
And first I beg thy Pardon,
And after that will get it from Clarina;
Which done, I'll wait upon thee to the Camp,
And suffer one year's Penance for this Sin,
Unless I could divert this Resolution,
By a Proposal Clarina bid me make you.

ALBERTO - What was it, Sir?

ANTONIO - I have a Sister, Friend, a handsome Virgin,
Rich, witty, and I think she's virtuous too;
Return'd last Week from St. Teresia's Monastery.

ALBERTO - Sure any thing that is to thee ally'd,
Must find a more than bare Respect from me;
But certain 'tis I ne'er shall love again,
And have resolv'd never to marry any,
Where Interest, and not Love, must join our hands.

ANTONIO - You cannot tell what Power there lies in Beauty;
Come, you shall see her, and if after that,
You find you cannot love her,
We'll both to Candia, where we both will prove
Rivals in Honour, as we're now in Love.
But I'ad forgot to tell thee what I came for;

I must this Evening beg your Company,
Nay, and perhaps your Sword: come along with me,
And by the way I'll tell you the Adventure.

[Exeunt.

SCENE III. The Lodgings of Curtius.

Enter Curtius and Pietro, disguis'd as before.

CURTIUS - I wonder we hear no news yet of the Prince,
I hope he'll come; Pietro, be the Bravoes ready,
And the Curtezans?

PIETRO - My Lord, they'll be here immediately, all well dress'd too.

CURTIUS - They be those Bravoes that belong to me?

PIETRO - Yes, Sir, the same;
But Antonio is their Patron.

CURTIUS - They be stout and secret; 'tis well,
Is the Music and all things ready?
For I'll not be seen till my Part is to be play'd.
What Arms have they?

PIETRO - Pistols, Sir, would you have other?

CURTIUS - No, I have not yet consider'd how to kill him,
Nor scarce resolv'd to do so any way.
What makes this strange Irresolution in me?
Sure 'tis the force of sacred Amity,
Which but too strictly was observ'd by me.
My Prince, and Friend, my Wife, and Sister too;
Shall not those last, the powerful first out-do?
My Honour, and my Love, are there ingag'd,
And here, by ties of Duty, I'm oblig'd:
I satisfy but these, if he must bleed;
But ruin the whole Dukedom in the Deed,
The hopeful Heir of all their noble Spoils,
And Joy and Recompence of all their Toils.
Why, so was Cloris, Laura too, to me,
Which both were ravish'd from me, Prince, by thee.   [Knocks within.

PIETRO - Sir, they be the Bravoes and Curtezans.   [Pietro goes out.

CURTIUS - 'Tis well, I need not talk with them,
They understand their work.

PIETRO - They do, my Lord, and shall be ready at your stamp;

They are all Neapolitans, you know, Sir.

CURTIUS - Are they the better for that?

PIETRO - Much, Sir, a Venetian will turn to your Enemy,
If he will give him but a Souse more than you have done;
And your Millanoise are fit for nothing but to
Rob the Post or Carrier; a Genovese too
Will sooner kill by Usury than Sword or Pistol;
A Roman fit for nothing but a Spy.

CURTIUS - Well, Sir, you are pleasant with my Countrymen.

PIETRO - I'll be so with my own too, Sir; and tell you,
That a Maltan, who pretends to so much Honour
And Gravity, are fit only to rob their Neighbours
With pretence of Piety,
And a Cicilian so taken up with Plots,
How to kill his Vice-Roy, that it keeps them
From being Rogues to a less degree.
But I have done, Sir, and beg your pardon.

CURTIUS - Didst leave the Letter, I commanded thee,
For Laura?

PIETRO - I did, my Lord.

Enter Lorenzo.

LORENZO - Well, here's the Prince just coming.

CURTIUS - Pray, Sir, conduct him in,
I'm ready for him.

[Ex. Curtius and Pietro.

Enter the Prince, conducted by two Women in Masquerade, with
Lights, he endeavouring to take off their Masks.

[Exit two Women.

[He walks about while this Song is singing.

What is the recompence of War,
But soft and wanton Peace?
What the best Balsam to our Scars,
But that which Venus gave to Mars,
When he was circled in a kind Embrace?

Behold a Prince, who never yet
Was vanquished in the Field;

Awhile his Glories must forget,
And lay his Laurels at the feet
Of some fair Female Power, to whom he'll yield.

FREDERICK - What's this the Preparation?

LORENZO - Yes, so it should seem; but had you met
With so many defeats as I have done to night,
You would willingly excuse this Ceremony.

Musick for the Dance.

Enter Antonio with Ismena, Alberto with Clarina, Laura and Cloris with two Men more, and all dress'd in Masquerade, with Vizards; they dance. The Prince sets down: the Dance being done, they retire to one side; and Alberto comes and presents him Clarina, and bows and retires; who puts off her Mask, and puts it on again, and retires.

FREDERICK - She's wondrous fair;
Sure in his whole Cabal he cannot show a fairer

LORENZO - She resembles Clarina; I wish your Highness
Would see further, and then perhaps this would
Fall to my lot, for I love her for likeness sake.
[Antonio presents Ismena, and retires as the other.

FREDERICK - This I confess out-does the others;
An Innocency dwells upon her Face,
That's strangely taking, is it not, Lorenzo?

LORENZO - To say truth, she is very fine indeed.
[They present Laura.

FREDERICK - Hah! I am amaz'd; see, Lorenzo,
Dost thou not know that Face?

LORENZO - O' my Conscience and Soul, 'tis my own Sister Laura;
Why, how now, Mistress,
Do things go thus with you, i'faith?
[She shakes her Hand, as not understanding him.

ANTONIO - Sir, she understands you not.

LORENZO - Is it not Laura then?

ANTONIO - No, Sir, it is a Stranger.

FREDERICK - Let her be what she will, I'll have her.
[FREDERICK - seems to talk, when she answers in Grimaces.

LORENZO - There have been Examples in the World
Of the good Offices done by a Brother to a Sister;

But they are very rare here,
And therefore will surely be the more acceptable.
Well, Sir, have you fix'd, that I may chuse?

FREDERICK - I have, and had he thousands more,   [Lorenzo goes to Clarina
I would refuse them all for this fair Creature.

Enter Pietro.

PIETRO - Sir, all things are ready as you desire,
But my Master must first speak with you alone.

FREDERICK - About the Price, I'll warrant you;
Let him come in: [All go out but Frederick, to him Curtius
Are you the Master of the Ceremony?

CURTIUS - I am.

FREDERICK - Be speedy then, and by my Impatiency
To be with that agreeable Stranger,
Guess at my Approbation of the Ladies, and which I chuse.

CURTIUS - Your mighty Heat, Sir, will be soon allay'd.

FREDERICK - Shall it?

CURTIUS - Yes, Sir, it shall, for you must die.

FREDERICK - Sure thou art mad to tell me so, whoe'er thou be'st,
Whilst I have this about me.   [Draws.

CURTIUS - That, Sir, you draw in vain; stand off -   [Offers a Pistol.

FREDERICK - What new conceited Preparation's this?

CURTIUS - Sir, when you know this Face, it will inform you.
[Pulls off his false Beard.

FREDERICK - Curtius! I am betray'd, oh Villain!   [Offers to fight.

CURTIUS - Ho, within there
[He calls, and all the masked Men come out, and offer their
Pistols at Frederick.

FREDERICK - Hold, I am the Prince of Florence.

CURTIUS - These, Sir, are Rogues, and have no sense of ought,
But Mischief in their Souls;
Gold is their Prince and God, go, be gone   [They withdraw.
See, Sir, I can command them.

FREDERICK - Curtius, why dost thou deal thus treacherously with me?
Did I not offer thee to fight thee fairly?

CURTIUS - 'Tis like the Injuries, Sir, that you have done me;
Pardon me if my Griefs make me too rude,
And in coarse terms lay all your Sins before you.
First, Sir, you have debauch'd my lovely Sister,
The only one I had;
The Hope and Care of all our noble Family:
Thou, Prince, didst ravish all her Virtue from her,
And left her nothing but a desperate sense of Shame,
Which only serv'd to do her self that Justice,
Which I had executed, had she not prevented me.

FREDERICK - In this, upon my Soul, you do me wrong.

CURTIUS - Next, (Oh, how unlike a brave and generous Man!)
Without a Cause, you cast me from your Bosom;
Withdrew the Honour of your promis'd Friendship,
And made me partner in my Sister's Fate;
Only with this difference, that she
You left to act a Murder on her self;
And mine you would have been so kind to've done
With your own hand, but my respect prevented it.
Next, Sir, you ravish'd Laura from me,
And under a pretence of sacred Friendship,
You prov'd your self the worst of Enemies;
And that's a Crime you dare not say was Ignorance,
As you perhaps will plead your Sin to Cloris was.

FREDERICK - Cloris, why, what hast thou to do with Cloris?

CURTIUS - She was my Sister, Frederick.

FREDERICK - Thy Sister!

CURTIUS - Yes, think of it well,
A Lady of as pure and noble Blood,
As that of the great Duke thy Father,
Till you, bad Man, infected it.
Say, should I murder you for this base Action,
Would you not call it a true Sacrifice?
And would not Heaven and Earth forgive it too?

FREDERICK - No, had I known that she had been thy Sister,
I had receiv'd her as a Gift from Heaven;
And so I would do still.

CURTIUS - She must be sent indeed from Heaven,
If you receive her now.

FREDERICK - Is Cloris dead? Oh, how I was to blame!   [Weeps.
Here thou mayst finish now the Life thou threaten'st.

CURTIUS - Now, Sir, you know my Justice and my Power;
Yet since my Prince can shed a Tear for Cloris,
I can forgive him; here, Sir, send me to Cloris,
[Kneels, and offers his Sword.
That Mercy possibly will redeem the rest
Of all the Wrongs you've done me;
And you shall find nothing but Sorrow here,
And a poor broken Heart that did adore you.

FREDERICK - Rise, Curtius, and divide my Dukedom with me;
Do any thing that may preserve thy Life,
And gain my Pardon; alas, thy Honour's safe,
Since yet none knows that Cloris was thy Sister,
Or if they do, I must proclaim this truth;
She dy'd thy Prince's Wife.

CURTIUS - These Tidings would be welcome to my Sister,
And I the fitting'st Man to bear that News.

[Offers to stab himself; is held by Frederick, Laura, and
Cloris, who come in with Isabella, dress'd like Philibert,
and the rest.

LAURA - Stay, Curtius, and take me with thee in the way.

CURTIUS - Laura, my dearest Laura! how came you hither?

LAURA - Commanded by your Letter; have you forgot it?

FREDERICK - Curtius, look here, is this not Cloris' Face?

CURTIUS - The same; Oh my sweet Sister, is it thee?
[Curtius goes to embrace her, she goes back.

FREDERICK - Do not be shy, my Soul, it is thy Brother.

CURTIUS - Yes, a Brother who despis'd his Life,
When he believ'd yours lost or sham'd:
But now the Prince will take a care of it.

CLORIS - May I believe my Soul so truly bless'd?

FREDERICK - Yes, Cloris, and thus low I beg thy pardon   [Kneels.
For all the Fears that I have made thee suffer.

Enter all the rest, first Antonio and Alberto, without their Vizors.

CLORIS - Rise, Sir, it is my Duty and my Glory.

ALBERTO - Sir, we have Pardons too to beg of you.

FREDERICK - Antonio and Alberto, what, turn'd Bravoes?

CURTIUS - I am amaz'd.

ANTONIO - You'll cease your Wonder, Sir, when you shall know,
Those Braves which formerly belong'd to you,
Are now maintain'd by me; which Pietro hir'd
For this night's service; and from them we learnt
What was to be done, (though not on whom)
But that we guess'd, and thought it but our duty
To put this Cheat on Curtius;
Which had we seen had been resolv'd to kill you,
Had been by us prevented:
The Ladies too would needs be Curtezans
To serve your Highness.

FREDERICK - I'm much oblig'd to them, as you.
Cloris, a while I'll leave thee with thy Brother,
Till I have reconcil'd thee to my Father:
To marry me, is what he long has wish'd for,
And will, I know, receive this News with Joy.   [Exit Prince.

LORENZO - Here's fine doings; what am I like to come to if he
Turn honest now? This is the worst piece of Inconstancy
He ever was guilty of; to change ones Humour, or so,
Sometimes, is nothing: but to change Nature,
To turn good on a sudden, and never give a Man
Civil warning, is a Defeat not be endur'd;
I'll see the end on't though.   [Goes out.

ALBERTO - Here, Antonio, imagine how I love thee,
Who make thee such a Present.

[Gives him Clarina, who is dressed just as Ismena was, and Ismena in a Masquing Habit.

ANTONIO - Clarina, can you pardon my Offence,
And bless me with that Love,
You have but justly taken from me?

CLARINA - You wrong me, Sir, I ne'er withdrew my Heart,
Though you, but too unkindly, did your Confidence.

ANTONIO - Do not upbraid me; that I was so to blame,
Is shame enough: pray pardon, and forget it.

CLARINA - I do.

ANTONIO - Alberto, to shew my Gratitude in what I may,

I beg you would receive Ismena from me.

ALBERTO - Who's this?

ANTONIO - Ismena, whom I promis'd thee.

ALBERTO - It is Clarina; do you mock my Pain?   [Shows Ismena.

ANTONIO - By Heaven, not I; this is Clarina, Sir.

ALBERTO - That thy Wife Clarina!
A Beauty which till now I never saw.

ANTONIO - Sure thou art mad, didst thou not give her me but now,
And hast not entertain'd her all this night?

ALBERTO - Her Habit and her Vizard did deceive me;
I took her for this lady, Oh bless'd Mistake!

ISMENA - I see you're in the dark, but I'll unfold the Riddle,
Sir, in the Passage from the Monastery,
Attended only by my Confessor,
A Gentleman, a Passenger, in the same Boat,
Address'd himself to me;
And made a many little Courtships to me:
I being veil'd, he knew not who receiv'd them,
Nor what Confusion they begot in me.
At the first sight, I grew to great esteems of him,
But when I heard him speak
I'm not asham'd to say he was my Conqueror.

ALBERTO - Oh, Madam, was it you?
Who by your Conversation in that Voyage,
Gave me Disquiets,
Which nothing but your Eyes could reconcile again?

ISMENA - 'Twas I whom you deceiv'd with some such Language.
After my coming home I grew more melancholy,
And by my silence did increase my Pain;
And soon Clarina found I was a Lover,
Which I confess'd at last, and nam'd the Object.
She told me of your Friendship with Antonio,
And gave me hopes that I again should see you:
But Isabella over-heard the Plot,
Which, Sir, Antonio did contrive with you,
To make a feigned Courtship to Clarina,
And told us all the story.

ALBERTO - Oh, how I'm ravish'd with my Happiness!

ISMENA - Clarina, Sir, at first was much inrag'd,

And vow'd she would revenge her on Antonio;
But I besought her to be pleas'd again,
And said I would contrive a Counter-Plot,
Should satisfy her Honour and Revenge.
Thus, Sir, I got a Garment like to hers;
And to be courted, though but in jest, by you,
I run all hazards of my Brother's Anger,
And your opinion of my Lightness too.

CLARINA - 'Twas a Temptation, Sir, I would not venture on,
Lest from the reasons of a just Revenge,
And so much Beauty as Alberto own'd,
My Virtue should not well secure your Interest.

ANTONIO - But why, Ismena, was that killing Plot,
When I was hid behind the Arras? for now I confess all.

ISMENA - To make Alberto confident of my Love,
And try his Friendship to the utmost point.
Alberto too I found had some reserves,
Which I believ'd his Amity to you.

ALBERTO - Yes, Madam, whilst I took you for his Wife,
I thought it crime enough but to adore you;
But now I may with honour own my Passion:
I will, Ismena, confidently assure you,
That I will die, unless you pity me.

ISMENA - She that durst tell you, Sir, how much she lov'd,
When you believ'd it was a Sin to do so,
Will now make good that Promise with Antonio's leave.

ANTONIO - With perfect Joy, Ismena, I resign thee,
[Antonio gives him Ismena

ALBERTO - By double Ties you now unite our Souls;
Though I can hardly credit what I see,
The Happiness so newly is arriv'd.   [To Antonio

Enter Prince, Lorenzo, and Guilliam, who comes up scraping to Cloris.

FREDERICK - My Father is the kindest Man on Earth,
And Cloris shall be welcome to his Bosom;
Who'll make him happy in my Reformation.
Here, Curtius, take Laura, who, I find,
Had rather be my Sister than my Mistress:
The Duke commands it so.

CURTIUS - Till you have pardon'd me my late Offences,
I must deny myself so great a Happiness.   [Curtius kneels.

FREDERICK - Rise, you have it.

Enter Salvator.

SALVATOR - Is here not a Runegado belongs to me?

LAURA - No, Sir, my Faith's entire,
And Curtius has the keeping of it.

SALVATOR - Who made him Master of it, hau?

LAURA - Heaven, my Inclinations and the Prince.

SALVATOR - Three powerful Opposers;
Take her, since it must be so,
And mayst thou be happy with her.

FREDERICK - Alberto, would this Court afforded
A Lady worthy thee.

ALBERTO - Sir, I'm already sped, I humbly thank you.

LORENZO - Sped, quoth ye? Heaven defend
Me from such Fortune.

FREDERICK - Lorenzo, I had forgot thee; thou shalt e'en marry too.

LORENZO - You may command me any thing but marrying.

ISABELLA - What think you then of a smooth-fac'd Boy?

LORENZO - A Pox on him, sure he will not tell now, will he?

ISABELLA - My Lord, I beg your leave to challenge Lorenzo.

FREDERICK - What, to a Duel, Philibert?

Lorenzo – Philbert. Philbert, hold, do not ruin the Reputation
Of a Man that has acquir'd Fame amongst the female Sex;
I protest I did but jest.

ISABELLA - But, Sir, I'm in earnest with you.

FREDERICK - This is not Philibert.

ISABELLA - No, Sir, but Isabella that was Philibert.
[Pointing to Cloris.

CLORIS - Yes, Sir, I was the happy Boy to be belov'd,
When Cloris was forgotten.

FREDERICK - Oh, how you raise my Love and Shame!
But why did Isabella change her Habit?

CLORIS - Only to take my place, lest you should miss me,
Who being with Laura, at the Lodgings of Clarina,
And comparing the Words of her Letter
With what the Bravoes had confess'd to Antonio,
We found the Plot which was laid for you,
And join'd all to prevent it.

FREDERICK - 'Twas sure the work of Heaven.

ISABELLA - And now, Sir, I come to claim a Husband here.

FREDERICK - Name him, and take him.

ISABELLA - Lorenzo, Sir.

LORENZO - Of all Cheats, commend me to a Waiting-Gentlewoman;
I her Husband?

ANTONIO - I am a Witness to that Truth.

FREDERICK - 'Tis plain against you; come, you must be honest.

LORENZO - Will you compel me to't against my will?
Oh Tyranny, consider, I am a Man of Quality and Fortune.

ISABELLA - As for my Qualities, you know I have sufficient,
And Fortune, thanks to your Bounty, considerable too.

FREDERICK - No matter, he has enough for both.

LORENZO - Nay, Sir, an you be against me,
'Tis time to reform in my own defence;
But 'tis a thing I never consider'd, or thought on.

FREDERICK - Marry first, and consider afterwards.

LORENZO - That's the usual way, I confess;
Come, Isabella, since the Prince commands it,
I do not love thee, but yet I'll not forswear it;
Since a greater Miracle than that is wrought,
And that's my marrying thee;
Well, 'tis well thou art none of the most beautiful,
I should swear the Prince had some designs on thee else.

CLORIS - Yes, Guilliam, since thou hast been so faithful,
I dare assure thee Lucia shall be thine.
[Cloris speaks aside to Guilliam. Guilliam bows.

FREDERICK - Come, my fair Cloris, and invest thy self
In all the Glories which I lately promis'd:
And, Ladies, you'll attend her to the Court,
And share the Welcomes which the Duke provides her;
Where all the Sallies of my flattering Youth
Shall be no more remember'd, but as past.
Since 'tis a Race that must by Man be run,
I'm happy in my Youth it was begun;
It serves my future Manhood to improve,
Which shall be sacrific'd to War and Love.

Curtain Falls.

EPILOGUE,

Spoken by Cloris.

Ladies, the Prince was kind at last,
But all the Danger is not past;
I cannot happy be till you approve
My hasty condescension to his Love.
'Twas want of Art, not Virtue, was my Crime;
And that's, I vow, the Author's Fault, not mine.
She might have made the Women pitiless,
But that had harder been to me than this:
She might have made our Lovers constant too,
A Work which Heaven it self can scarcely do;
But simple Nature never taught the way
To hide those Passions which she must obey.
E'en humble Cottages and Cells,
Where Innocence and Virtue dwells,
Than Courts no more secure can be
From Love and dangerous Flattery.
Love in rural Triumph reigns,
As much a God amongst the Swains,
As if the Sacrifices paid
Were wounded Hearts by Monarchs made:
And this might well excuse th' Offence,
If it be so to love a Prince.
But, Ladies, 'tis your Hands alone,
And not his Power, can raise me to a Throne;
Without that Aid I cannot reign,
But will return back to my Flocks again.

Guilliam advances.

GUILLIAM - How, go from Court! nay, zay not zo.
Hear me but speak before you go:
Whoy zay the Leadies should refuse ye,

The Bleads I'm sure would better use ye
So long as ye are kind and young,
I know they'll clap ye right or wrong.

Aphra Behn – A Short Biography

Aphra Behn was baptised on December 14th in 1640.

Although she was a prolific and well established writer in her own lifetime facts about her remain scant and difficult to confirm. What can safely be said though is that Aphra Behn is now regarded as a key English playwright and a major figure in Restoration theatre

In fact even where and to whom she was born are subject to discussion.

According to which account you read – and there are many – Aphra was born in Harbledown, near Canterbury. Another that she was born to a barber, John Amis and his wife Amy. Or again she was born to a couple named Cooper.

In the "The Histories And Novels of the Late Ingenious Mrs. Behn" (1696) it is written that Aphra was born to Bartholomew Johnson, a barber, and Elizabeth Denham, a wet-nurse. However a claim by Colonel Thomas Colepeper, who states he knew her as a child, wrote in Adversaria that she was born at "Sturry or Canterbury" to a Mr Johnson and that she had a sister named Frances. Anne Kingsmill Finch, Countess of Winchilsea, a poetic contemporary, says that Aphra was born in Wye in Kent, and was the 'Daughter to a Barber.'

None of these accounts can be relied upon and it follows that with so few facts the early part of her life cannot be clearly illustrated.

However what can be accurately suggested is that Aphra was born in the rising tensions to the English Civil War. Obviously a time of much division and difficulty as the King and Parliament, and their respective forces, came ever closer to conflict.

But still facts do not reveal themselves in any quantity. As a young woman a version exists of Aphra's journeying to Surinam with Bartholomew Johnson. He was said to have died on the journey, leaving his wife and children spending some months in the country. It is during this trip that Aphra claims to have met an African slave leader. These experiences formed the basis for one of her most famous works, "Oroonoko". In "Oroonoko" Behn Aphra gifts herself the position of narrator and her first biographer accepted the proposition that Aphra was indeed the daughter of the lieutenant general of Surinam, as in the story. There is little evidence to support this case, and none of her contemporaries acknowledge this, or any, aristocratic status. There is also no evidence that Oroonoko existed as an actual person or that any such slave revolt, is anything but an invention.

However it is possible that she acted a spy in the colony. Possibilities exist. Perhaps Aphra re-wrote her own history as and when it suited her needs at the time.

The common method of gathering information in these times was Church records and for a few, tax records. Aphra Behn is mentioned in neither. As well as Aphra Behn or Mrs Behn she was, at times, also known as Ann Behn, Mrs Bean, agent 160 and Astrea.

Shortly after her supposed return to England from Surinam in 1664, Aphra may have married Johan Behn (also written as Johann and John Behn). He could have been a merchant of German or Dutch extraction, possibly from Hamburg. He died or the couple separated that same year, however from this point we can be sure Aphra used the title "Mrs Behn" as her professional name.

There is some suggestion that Aphra may have been a Catholic or at least leaned towards this school of faith. She once commented that she was "designed for a nun." Many of those around her were Catholic, such as Henry Neville who was later arrested for his Catholicism, and this would have aroused suspicions during the anti-Catholic fervour of the 1680s. She was a monarchist, and her sympathy for the Stuarts, and particularly for the Catholic Duke of York may be demonstrated by her dedication of her play "The Rover, Part II" to him after he had been exiled for the second time. Aphra was dedicated to the restored King Charles II. As political parties emerged during this time, Aphra became a Tory supporter.

By 1666 Aphra had become attached to the court. Domestically the Plague was sweeping the Nation and the Great Fire was about to erupt through London. In foreign affairs England and the Netherlands had engaged in The Second Anglo-Dutch War from 1665. Aphra was recruited as a political spy in Antwerp on behalf of King Charles II, possibly in league with Thomas Killigrew.

This is probably the beginning of more accurate records on Aphra's life. Her code name is said to have been Astrea (though there are others), a name under which she later published many of her writings. Her chief duty was to establish a relationship with William Scot, son of Thomas Scot, a regicide who had been executed in 1660. Scot was believed to be ready to become a spy in the English service and to report on the activities of the English exiles who were thought to be plotting against the King. Aphra arrived in Bruges in July 1666 with a mission to secure Scot into a double agent, but there is evidence that Scot would betray her to the Dutch.

Aphra however found life as a spy not quite the romantic interlude that many assume would be the case. She arrived unprepared; the cost of living shocked her, and after a month, she had to pawn her jewellery. King Charles was slow in paying, either for her services or for her expenses whilst abroad. She had to borrow money so she could return to London, where she spent a year petitioning King Charles for payment unsuccessfully. A short while later a warrant was issued for her arrest, but little to suggest it was actually served or that she went to prison for her debt.

The death of her husband and her debts seemed to push her towards a more sustainable and substantial career. Aphra began work for the King's Company and the Duke's Company players as a scribe. These were, in fact, the only two licensed theatre groups in London. The theatres had been closed under Cromwell and were now re-opening under Charles II and a more liberal atmosphere. Theatre technology was being imported from Europe and being integrated into the staging of some plays. It was a great moment on which to embark upon a career in theatre.

Aphra who had previously only written poetry now embarked on such a career. Her first, "The Forc'd Marriage", was staged in 1670, followed by "The Amorous Prince" (1671). After her third play, "The Dutch Lover", fails to please Aphra had a three year lull in her writing career. Again it is speculated that she went travelling again, possibly once again as a spy.

After this sojourn her writing moves towards comic works, which prove commercially more successful. Her most popular works included "The Rover" and "Love-Letters Between a Nobleman and His Sister" (1684–87).

With her growing reputation Aphra became friends with many of the most notable writers of the day. This is The Age of Dryden and his literary dominance. As well as his friendship she includes also those of Elizabeth Barry, John Hoyle, Thomas Otway and Edward Ravenscroft, and was also attached to the circle of the Earl of Rochester.

Aphra often used her plays to attack the parliamentary Whigs claiming, "In public spirits call'd, good o' th' Commonwealth... So tho' by different ways the fever seize...in all 'tis one and the same mad disease." This was Aphra's criticism to parliament which had denied the king funds.

From the mid 1680's Aphra's health began to decline. This was exacerbated by her continual state of debt and descent into poverty.

In 1687 she published A Discovery of New Worlds, a translation of a French popularisation of astronomy, Entretiens sur la pluralité des mondes, by Bernard le Bovier de Fontenelle, written as a novel in a form similar to her own work, but with her new, religiously oriented preface.

As her end approached in 1689 it became increasingly hard for her to even hold a pen though her desire to continue to write was unquenchable. In her final days, she wrote the translation of the final book of Abraham Cowley's Six Books of Plants.

Aphra Behn died on April 16th 1689, and is buried in the East Cloister of Westminster Abbey. The inscription on her tombstone reads: "Here lies a Proof that Wit can never be Defence enough against Mortality." She was quoted as stating that she had led a "life dedicated to pleasure and poetry."

Her legacy is broad. Firstly as a woman she broke down many of the barriers which regarded only men as writers, especially in the commercial arena. In all she would write and have performed 19 plays, contribute to more, and become one of the first prolific, high-profile female dramatists in these Isles.

In her own golden age of the 1670s and 1680s she was one of the most productive playwrights in Britain, second only to the immense talents of the Poet Laureate John Dryden.

Much of her work has been criticised for its bawdy tone as well as its masculine form but needs must and she was working to live, to survive, and to widen her spread as an author.

She received widespread support from many other successful writers including Thomas Otway, Nahum Tate (also a Poet Laureate), Jacob Tonson, Nathaniel Lee and Thomas Creech.

Aphra is now rightly seen as a key dramatist of the seventeenth-century theatre. Her prose vitally important to the on-going development of the English novel.

Following Aphra's death new female dramatists such as 'Ariadne', Delarivier Manley, Mary Fix, Susanna Centlivre and Catherine Trotter acknowledged Behn as an inspiration who opened up the public space for women writers to be accepted.

In succeeding centuries her appreciation has been volatile. For instance in the morally reserved Victorian clime both the writer and her works were ignored or dismissed as indecent. The Victorian novelist and critic Julia Kavanagh wrote, "the disgrace of Aphra Behn is that, instead of raising man to woman's moral standard, she sank woman to the level of man's coarseness".

However by the 20th century, however, Aphra's fame was back in fashion. Since then her works have been well appreciated and her place in our literary pantheon assured.

Aphra Behn – A Concise Bibliography

Plays
The Forced Marriage (1670)
The Amorous Prince (1671)
The Dutch Lover (1673)
Abdelazer (1676)
The Town Fop (1676)
The Rover, Part I (1677)
Sir Patient Fancy (1678)
The Feigned Courtesans (1679)
The Young King (1679)
The False Count (1681)
The Rover, Part II (1681)
The Roundheads (1681)
The City Heiress (1682)
Like Father, Like Son (1682)
Prologue and Epilogue to Romulus and Hersilia, or The Sabine War (November 1682)
The Lucky Chance (1686) with composer John Blow
The Emperor of the Moon (1687)
The Widow Ranter (1689)
The Younger Brother (1696)

Novels
The Fair Jilt
Agnes de Castro
Love-Letters Between a Nobleman and His Sister (1684)
Oroonoko (1688)

Short Stories
The Fair Jilt (1688)
The History of the Nun: or, the Fair Vow-Breaker (1688)
The History of the Servant
The Lover-Boy of Germany
The Girl Who Loved the German Lover-Boy

Poetry Collections
Poems upon Several Occasions, with A Voyage to the Island of Love (1684)
Lycidus; or, The Lover in Fashion (1688)

The Dorset Square Theatre – A Short History

Many of Aphra Behn's plays were first performed at the Dorset Garden Theatre in London which was originally built in 1671.

The theatre itself is rich in history though it survived for less than forty years. In its first years it was also commonly called the Duke of York's Theatre, as well as the Duke's Theatre. Charles II died in 1685 and his brother the Duke of York was crowned King James II. The theatre then changed its name to The Queen's Theatre in honour of James' wife Mary of Modena.

It was the fourth home of the Duke's Company, one of the two patent theatre companies in Restoration London, and after 1682 continued to be used by the company's successor, the United Company.

After the Civil war and the harsh years of the Interregnum the ban on theatres was lifted with the Restoration of Charles II in 1660. He granted Letters Patent to two theatre companies. One enjoyed his own patronage, this was 'The King's Company'. The other was patronised by his brother the Duke of York and was known as The Duke's Company.

Both were originally based in the Cockpit Theatre, an old Jacobean theatre in Drury Lane. The Duke's Company then moved for a short time to the Salisbury Court Theatre and thence in 1662 to Portugal Street in Lincoln's Inn Fields remaining there until 1671. The King's Company meanwhile moved to the Theatre Royal, Drury Lane.

Sir William Davenant, the respected Poet Laureate, founded the Duke's company and brought much innovation to theatre especially with regard to changeable scenery and theatrical machinery. Davenant died on April 7th 1668. He had made plans for a new theatre but died before ground was broken on the new theatre in 1670. This was funded to the tune of £9,000 by the Davenant family, the theatre's leading actor Thomas Betterton and others. A site was leased in Dorset Square under a 39 year lease at a rent of £130.55 per annum.

The theatre opened in the following year with the return of Thomas Betterton to England from a trip to France. It is thought that Betterton had gone several times over the years to bring back French thinking and equipment and certainly this seems evident with the Company's elaborate productions, including operatic adaptations of Shakespeare's Macbeth (1673), The Tempest (1674), and Thomas Shadwell's Pysche (1675). These productions employed changeable perspective scenery moved by machines as well as for flying actors and objects

The site of the theatre, was in the former grounds of Dorset House, London seat of the Sackville Earls of Dorset. Destroyed in the Great Fire of London it was soon densely built over with speculative tenements. It appears part of the site had been used as a theatre in the time of Charles I: in 1629 the Earl of Dorset leased the "stables and out howses towards the water side" behind Dorset House... to make a playhouse for the children of the revels."

The site for the new theatre, by Dorset Stairs in Whitefriars on the Thames, was slightly upstream from the outlet of the New Canal, part of the Fleet River. Its position on the Thames permitted the patrons to travel to the theatre by boat, avoiding the nearby crime-ridden neighbourhood of Alsatia. It opened on 9 November 1671 and was almost twice the size of the Duke's Company's former theatre. It became the principal playhouse in London when the Theatre Royal burned down in January 1672, and only rivalled when the new Theatre Royal opened in March 1674.

After the Duke's Company merged with the King's Company in 1682 to form the United Company, the theatre in Dorset Garden was used mainly for opera, music, and spectaculars. From the 1690s it was used as well for other entertainments, such as weight lifting, until it was demolished in 1709.

Apart from the illustrations in the libretto of The Empress of Morocco, no contemporary pictures of the interior are known. It is thought that the interior was richly decorated: the proscenium arch had carvings by Grinling Gibbons.

The Dorset Garden theatre, typically for English theatres, had a large forestage. Edward Langhans in his reconstruction calculated the forestage to be 19'6" feet deep and 30'6" wide at the proscenium arch. This forestage provided actors, singers and dancers with a sizeable downstage and a well lit performance space, free of grooves. When a locale was depicted by the scenery, the forestage was understood to be an extension of that place and served as the link between the audience and the performers, the auditorium and the stage, the playgoers and the play.

Access to the forestage was by proscenium doors, probably two on each side of the stage. Above the doors were balconies; acting spaces that could also serve for seating.

The scenic stage was probably some 50' deep and 30' high. The proscenium arch may have been some 30' wide and at least 25' high to accommodate the scenery in operas such as Dioclesian, The Fairy-Queen, or The World in the Moon. Both the forestage and the scenic stage were raked. The music box above the proscenium arch could hold perhaps 8 to 10 musicians, to provide incidental music. A full orchestra would be sitting in the pit, just in front of the stage.

The Duke's Company had already been using moveable scenery to good effect in their previous playhouses. It was first employed by Davenant at Rutland House, using shutters in grooves, which could be slid open or closed to reveal a new scene. However Dorset Garden was also equipped to fly at least four separate people and large objects like a cloud covering the full width of the stage and carrying a large group of musicians (such as in Psyche 1675). There were also numerous floor traps. It was primarily designed for staging Restoration spectaculars, and was the only playhouse in London capable of all the effects these lavish and exuberant spectacles required.

It is not known who designed the new theatre building. On the outside it measured 148' by 57', including a 10' deep porch.

A foreign visitor reported in 1676 that it contained a central "pit", in the form of an amphitheatre, two tiers of seven boxes each holding twenty people, and an upper gallery. In all the theatre could entertain 850 people at a time. The theatre represented a great investment to the Duke's Company. Thomas Betterton lived in an apartment on an upper floor on the south side. And living nearby were such luminaries as Aphra Behn in Dorset Street; John Dryden in Salisbury Square (from 1673 to 1682) and John Locke in Dorset Court in 1690.

www.ingramcontent.com/pod-product-compliance
Lightning Source LLC
Chambersburg PA
CBHW061459040426
42450CB00008B/1419